Chauncey Giles

**Perfect prayer**

How offered, how answered

Chauncey Giles

**Perfect prayer**
*How offered, how answered*

ISBN/EAN: 9783337283841

Printed in Europe, USA, Canada, Australia, Japan

Cover: Foto ©Lupo / pixelio.de

More available books at **www.hansebooks.com**

# PERFECT PRAYER

## HOW OFFERED: HOW ANSWERED.

BY

### REV. CHAUNCEY GILES.

"Teach us to pray."—LUKE ii. 1.

PHILADELPHIA:

J. B. LIPPINCOTT & CO.

1883.

# CONTENTS.

# INTRODUCTION.

THE use of Prayer and the manner in which it operates to produce its effects is a subject which has awakened unusual interest in the Christian world in the last few years. As men become better acquainted with the substances and forces of the material world they see more clearly that all things proceed according to immutable laws. Storms, droughts, wars, famines, and pestilences, which it was formerly believed were sent upon men by an angry God to punish them for their sins, are now seen to be the effects of natural causes which are constant in their operation, and which in a great degree are under human control. Why, then, should we ask the Lord to interpose and prevent effects which His own forces acting according to His own laws produce? Why should we ask the Lord to save us from the consequences of our own wicked actions, when it can only be done by a change in ourselves? The more clearly men see that human suffering is due to their own ignorance of the laws of life, or to their wilful disobedience to them, the more they will be disposed to doubt the propriety of asking the Lord to avert a calamity which is caused by a violation of the laws and order of infinite wisdom.

All the happiness and blessings we enjoy are also the effect of immutable causes. Man was made for happiness. All his faculties of body and spirit are organized to be the subjects of pleasurable sensations and the most exquisite joys, and all the forms and forces of the material and spiritual worlds are adjusted to this infinitely complex organization with the most delicate and the most exact precision for the purpose of ministering to human happiness, the essential purpose for which the Lord works. Why, then, should we ask the Lord to do that for ourselves or others which He is in the constant effort to do? He regards us with infinite love now; can any appeal from human lips move Him to an intenser love? He is employing all the means in His infinite power directed by His infinite wisdom for our highest good now; can He be persuaded to do more or better by our importunities? It is impossible in the nature of things. Why, then, should we pray? The answer evidently must be that our asking is one of the means, one link in the chain of causes and effects by which the evil is averted or the good bestowed.

Another cause of doubt about the efficacy of prayer lies in the fact that many earnest and importunate prayers are not granted. The Lord says to men, " Ask and it shall be given to you." Humble and sincere Christians do ask, in words at least, and their request is not granted. Then doubts of many kinds arise. Does not the Lord keep His promises? Is there any use in asking if there is no certainty of receiving an answer? It is generally supposed that the Lord can grant our requests immediately by a direct exercise of omnipotent power, and when the answer does not come we fall into doubt about His willingness or power to do it. Yet He may be answering us the most directly even when He seems to be deaf to our entreaties. There may be obstacles in the way of which we have no knowledge, which can only be removed according to the laws of the Divine order and with our co-operation, and it may require much progress in spiritual life before we are willing to give that.

There is a prevalent misconception about the end to be obtained by prayer. It is generally supposed that the office of prayer consists in working some change in the mind of the Lord by which He can be induced to save us from evils, or grant us blessings which He would not otherwise have done. But this cannot be its purpose. There is no necessity for any change in Him. The only permanent obstacles to our complete happiness lie in ourselves; consequently the only change required is in ourselves, and the principal use of prayer is its agency in bringing us into a state in which the Lord can save and bless us. It has been objected with much emphasis to this view of the purpose of prayer that it makes our petitions a mere pretense. We ask the Lord to render us a service which we know He desires to grant; we implore a gift which we refuse to receive when offered to us. But even when we know this we may be sincere in our petitions, because we need Divine aid to remove the obstacles which exist in our own minds, as much as to bestow the gift. In all genuine prayer there is behind the special request an acknowledgment of our dependence upon the Lord for the power to receive as well as to ask, and a surrender of the inmost causes of thought and affection to His guidance. However desirable the special blessing we seek may seem to us, the condition " not as I will, but as Thou wilt," is always implied. Sincere, genuine prayer tends to bring us into such relations to the Lord that we can receive what He gives us the power to ask. It is a state of humiliation in which our own evil desires are held in abeyance; it is turning to the Lord and opening our affections to a fuller reception of the Divine life; it is yielding ourselves up in affection and thought to the Divine guidance. So far as we do this we come within the sphere of the Divine power, and the Lord can do more for us than we can ask or conceive.

It is the aim of the author of the following pages to give the answer of the New Church to some of the questions which are now frequently asked concerning the nature and use of prayer, to show in what genuine prayer essentially consists, and to set forth the conditions on which it can be answered. It will be seen that much stress is laid upon the fact that man is only a form capable of receiving life, and consequently that his essential relation to the Lord is that of a recipient of life to the Giver of it. This central truth is the key to some of the most difficult problems of existence. It shows us that prayer is not merely a matter of words, that it is an actual turning to the Source of life, and the opening of the organic forms of the mind to its influx. The discourses were first published separately as they were delivered, and in that form they have been widely circulated. So many acknowledgments have been received from inquiring and devout minds of the help they have derived from them in removing their doubts about the efficacy of prayer, and in gaining assurance that every genuine prayer will be answered when the conditions are fulfilled on which the Lord's promises are made, that it is hoped their use may be continued by publication in a more permanent form. In the exposition of the " perfect prayer" which our Lord gives to all who come to Him with the request, " teach us to pray," it has been the endeavor to give some help in raising it above a mere formality, to show the richness of its vital power and its perfect adaptation to all human needs. Infinite Wisdom is its author, and it must contain infinite treasures of goodness and truth. That all who are seeking a heavenly life and a more intimate communion with the Lord may find some assistance in the following pages, is the sincere prayer of the

AUTHOR.

# I

# EFFICACIOUS PRAYER.

---

*" If ye shall ask anything in my name, I will do it."*—
John xiv. 14.

THE nature and use of prayer is a living question. It touches the hopes and fears, the customs and the heart, of humanity. All religions, Christian and Pagan alike, teach the duty and the use of prayer. The Sacred Scriptures of both the Old and New Testaments commend it by example, enforce it by precept, encourage it by promises, and illustrate its nature and use by numerous and impressive examples. Our Lord taught His disciples how to pray, exhorted them to do it earnestly and faithfully, encouraged them by the most solemn promises of a full and speedy answer, and gave to them and to the world His own Divine example. He prayed often with fervor and sometimes with agony. Surely there is testimony sufficient to show the nature and use of prayer and to incite to its faithful practice. It is a want implanted in the human mind; it is in harmony with the laws of the Divine order.

But still there are many doubts about its efficacy. Multitudes of apparently sincere and fervent prayers are not answered. We are brought face to face with this question

11

to-day in a direct and forcible manner.  Millions of sincere and earnest prayers, from day to day and week to
week, were offered to the Lord to preserve the life of
our beloved President.  Days were set apart and specially
dedicated to this service by our public magistrates.  Christians in foreign lands united in the petition.  It is hardly
an exaggeration to say that the whole Christian world 'was
on its knees before the throne of grace, imploring the
mercy of our Heavenly Father to spare this precious life
to us.  But the prayer was not answered in the sense it
was generally offered.  After a long and painful struggle
the illustrious martyr passed away from earth to his final
home.  Why was not the prayer of so many millions of
people answered?  The prayers were sincere, fervent, for a
noble purpose, and oft-repeated.  Such a conspicuous instance of the apparent inefficacy of prayer cannot fail to
awaken doubts in the minds of many sincere Christians,
even about its use and power to prevail with the Lord.
These doubts ought, if possible, to be removed, for they
tend to unsettle the faith of man in the Divine Providence,
in the goodness and mercy of the Lord, and in His faith-
fulness in keeping His promises.

The Lord promises to answer prayer.  These promises
are direct, positive, and repeatedly made in the most solemn
manner.  The Old Testament is full of such promises.
They are reiterated, if possible, with more emphasis and
solemnity in the New.  The Lord calls Himself the hearer
of prayer.  His ears are ever open to the cry of His
people.  He encourages us to ask freely, fully.  " I say
unto you," He says, " Ask, and it shall be given unto
you."  " For every one that asketh receiveth."  " If ye
shall ask anything in my name, I will do it."  " If ye

abide in me, and my words abide in you, ye shall ask what ye will and it shall be done unto you." "Ask, and ye shall receive, that your joy may be full." We, are invited, exhorted to ask, and the promise is explicit that we shall receive what we ask for. But oftener than otherwise our prayer is not, or does not seem to be answered. Why is it? Does not the Lord keep His promise? Before we answer that question in the negative we ought to examine the question in all its bearings. We ought to be sure that we ask. Prayer is asking.

What is asking? It must be something more than repeating a prayer by rote; something more than articulate breath. Millions of prayers may be repeated without asking a favor of the Lord. The words employed are empty sounds. They are not the expression of any desire; they are not the form of any thought. Asking is turning to the Lord, opening the heart to Him. It is the turning of the soul to the Lord and the opening of its inmost forms to the quickening breath of the Holy Spirit, as the plant turns to the sun and opens every cell and pore to the light and to the quickening breath of his heat. Genuine prayer is not merely a matter of terms. We may use the most appropriate and eloquent words and not ask for a blessing. On the other hand, we may ask in the most effective form and not utter a sound. The will and the affections may lie prostrate in profound humiliation and entire self-surrender to the Lord to be penetrated by His life, and led by His wisdom. The heart asks, and He who looks upon the heart sees the desire before it is formed into thought. He hears the cry of the spirit before it gains vocal utterance, and answers before we call. We find in the body perfect examples of real asking. As

hunger is the body's prayer for bread; thirst, its prayer
for water; so desire is the soul's prayer for the means to
satisfy its wants.

There is often entire contrariety between the prayer of
the heart and the prayer of the lips. We do not desire
what we formally ask, and we would stoutly resist receiving it if it were offered to us. How many millions of
men and women will repeat the Divine petitions to-day,
"Thy kingdom come. Forgive us our trespasses as we forgive those who trespass against us," while they are opposing the coming of the Lord's kingdom in their own hearts,
and in the world! If it should come, and the Lord's will
should be done on the earth as it is in heaven, it would
defeat their purposes, destroy their business, blast their
hopes. How many would dare to ask the Lord to forgive
them *as* they forgive others? As much, and no more.
Would it not be equivalent to asking Him not to forgive
them? Genuine, complete, effective asking is an action
of the whole nature; it is the consenting voice of every
faculty. It begins in the heart, it is formed in the understanding, it is merely expressed with the lips.

Such being the nature of genuine prayer, let us consider
the conditions on which it is answered. Every Divine
promise is made upon conditions, and no prayer can be answered unless those conditions are complied with. These
conditions are always the same, though variously expressed.
At one time the condition is faith, "Whatsoever things
ye desire, when ye pray, believe that ye receive them and
ye shall have them." "All things are possible to him that
believeth." The condition on which our Lord wrought
His miracles of healing was faith in Him. "Believest
thou that I can do this?" was almost invariably His ques-

tion. "He did not many mighty works" in His own country, "because of their unbelief."

In our text asking in His name is the condition. What are we to understand by His "name"? There has been the most remarkable misconception by religious teachers of what is meant in this and many other passages by the "name" of the Lord. It has been supposed that it meant "for His sake." Consequently, prayer is generally addressed to the Father, and He is asked to grant the petition for the sake of the Son. In this way two distinct persons are recognized as God, and one is asked to grant a favor, not because He delights to confer blessings upon man, which He must do if He is a being of infinite love; not for man's sake, because he is poor and perishing and needs Divine mercy and aid; but for the sake of His Son. There is but one instance in the whole Bible where it is said that God confers any blessing upon men for Christ's sake, and that is a mistranslation, which is corrected in the new revision. In this passage the Apostle exhorts the Ephesians to forgive one another even as God " in Christ," which is true doctrine, " has forgiven them," and not as in the old version, " for Christ's sake," which is neither Scripture nor true doctrine.

A glance at the use of "name" in the sacred Scriptures will show that it must mean more than a mere epithet applied to the Lord, as we give names to children. One of the commandments forbids us " to take the Lord's name in vain." The Lord warns the children of Israel to beware of the Angel whom He would send before them, "for," He says, "my name is in him." They are repeatedly forbidden to profane His holy name. Solomon built a house unto the name of the Lord. The Psalms and prophets are full of similar expressions. The Lord is implored to pardon, to quicken, to bless for His name's sake. The Psalmist calls upon men to honor, praise, glorify, and bless the Lord's holy name. Our Saviour taught His disciples to pray " Hallowed be thy name." He calls His own sheep by name, writes His name upon their foreheads, gives to His people a new name. They who believe will have life in His name. These and a multitude of other passages show that name stands for the Lord Himself. It involves all the Divine attributes, and embodies all the laws of the Divine order. It comprehends His love, wisdom, power, and all the methods of carrying His purposes of good to men into effect.

To ask in His name, therefore, is to ask according to His will and wisdom. It is to ask that the Lord shall decide whether the request itself is a wise one, and whether it will be for our good, or not, to have it answered in our own way. We are always asking for favors which it would be to our injury, and to the injury of others, to have granted. We ask for success in every undertaking; for exemption from all pain and sorrow ; for wealth, pleasure, ·honor, power. But all these attainments for every one are impossible in the nature of human society. We do not ask them in the name of the Lord ; we ask them in our own name; according to our desires, and the measure of our wisdom, or the degree of our folly.

The conditions on which we shall receive what we ask are expressed in another way, which throws much light upon the subject. Our Lord compares His relation to men to that which exists between the vine and its branches. " I am the vine," He says, " ye are the branches." " If ye abide in me, and my words abide in you, ye shall ask what ye will and it shall be done unto you." Here the conditions of obtaining whatever we ask are, " If ye abide in me, and my words abide in you." They are without doubt the same as asking in His name, and believing in Him with undoubting faith. No one truly believes in the Lord who does not abide in Him, and in whom the Lord's words do not abide. Nor can any others ask in His name, because they do not know what it is. Here, then, we have the conditions on which the Lord promises to answer prayer, and the only conditions on which He can give us what we ask. They are that the request shall be in accord with all the laws of the Divine order, and the purposes of infinite love and wisdom.

It is absurd to suppose that He would answer any other petitions, or could grant our requests in any other way. A wise parent will not grant the request of the child he loves, even though it would give him great present satisfaction, and save from momentary pain, if he knows that it would harm the child. If it were necessary that a broken bone should be set, or a limb amputated, to prevent lasting deformity, or to save the child's life, he would insist on the operation, however earnestly the child might plead against it, because he loves his child, and looks to its permanent and greatest good. Is it not absurd to suppose that the Lord, who sees the end in the beginning, who knows the bearing of success and defeat, of joy and sorrow, upon individual and national happiness, should grant every request which men, who are blinded by selfish and worldly affections, and who judge mostly by appearances, may make? Will He annul or suspend the laws of His Divine order, and act contrary to the ordinations of His Divine Providence, at the request of one man or of a mil-

2

lion of men? How could He govern the universe and preserve order in its movements if He did? Large bodies of men often pray for directly opposite things. Two nations are at war. Each one prays for its own success. Both are equally fervent and sincere, and have equal faith. To grant the prayers of one nation would be to reject the petitions of the other. It would be impossible to grant the prayers of both. The Lord does not promise to answer every prayer. He only promises to answer those which accord with certain prescribed conditions.

These conditions operate in two ways. They determine the nature of the request, as well as of the answer. Our prayers are the outgrowth and expression of ourselves. They depend upon our character, our intelligence, our purposes in life. We ask only for those things which we believe to be favorable to us. We seek escape from some impending calamity, or for the bestowal of some fancied good. But what we regarded as a calamity might prove a blessing, and the seeming good might prove to be a curse. Every affection asks for gratification. A wicked man will not ask for the same things as a good man. One who is ignorant of the Lord, or who has misconceptions of His true character, will not pray in the same way, or for the same objects as the man who has some true knowledge of Him and His laws. The man who believes that the Lord is a being of infinite love who only seeks to bless His children, will not pray to be saved from His wrath, for He knows that He has none. He will not implore in abject fear the Lord to have mercy upon him, for he knows that He is in the constant effort to do it. The history of religions, and our own experience, show that what men desire and pray for is determined by their own knowledge and character.

When we abide in the Lord and His words abide in us we shall be filled with His love; we shall be imbued with His spirit; we shall be directed by His wisdom; His way will be our way. As His words abide in us, they will become the living springs of our action. We shall desire to have no will or way of our own which is contrary to His will. Would it be possible for a man in this state to ask for the gratification of any selfish desire? It would be contrary to every principle of his nature. His mind could not conceive such a prayer; his lips could not utter it. Could he ask, without reservation, to be released from any labor, to be saved from any trial, however strongly he may shrink from it? We cannot help shrinking from pain and suffering of every kind; and when the suffering is great we cannot restrain a desire to be free from it. Our Lord Himself did. But it may be for our good to suffer it, and, therefore, from a higher point of view, we could not ask to be saved from it. When in more than mortal agony our Lord prayed, "O my Father, if it be possible, let this cup pass from me," He added, "Nevertheless not as I will, but as Thou wilt." "If we abide in Him, and His words abide in us," we can pray in no other way. Every prayer will be put up in the spirit, and with the reservation, "Not as I will, but as Thou wilt." As we come into union with the Lord, and are imbued with His spirit, and trust Him with implicit confidence, we shall have no desire for anything contrary to His will. The quality of our prayers will change. We shall only ask directly and positively for spiritual good; for help to overcome our evils; for light in our darkness, and for the love of heaven in our hearts. If we pray for particular, natural blessings, or to be saved from the difficulties and dan-

gers and trials of this life, it will always be with the reservation, "Nevertheless not my will, but Thine be done."
So far as we cherish this spirit, and pray in this manner,
our request will be answered.

In the light of these principles let us look at some re-
cent events in our own history. Probably no more sincere,
fervent, and persistent prayers were ever offered to the
Lord for any special favor than that the life of our late
President should be spared to the nation. So far as these
petitions were offered up in the name of the Lord they
were granted, so far as they did not comply with those
conditions they were not granted. How can this be, it
will be asked, when both prayed for the same thing? But
both classes did not pray for the same thing. There was
the widest difference in their requests,—difference in
principle, and in the object sought. Both parties agree
in one point, that the life of the President may be spared;
but one class asks that it may be done, *if it be consistent
with the laws of the Divine order, and the highest good of
our nation, and of the world.* Their prayer is breathed
in the Lord's name, and with the implied reservation,
"Nevertheless not as I will, but as Thou wilt." The real
prayer is that the Lord will do what in His infinite wisdom
He sees to be best. The answer is left with Him. Their
prayer is answered, is it not? The Lord has done what
in His infinite wisdom He knew to be best for our nation,
for our beloved President, for his family, and for the world.
His wound was mortal. All the forces stored up by the
Divine Providence in his mind and body, in the skill of
his physicians, and in the remedies applied for his relief,
were not sufficient to save him. His life could only have
been prolonged by a violation of the laws of the Divine

wisdom; and that was not asked for by those who prayed in the Lord's name. They did not ask Him to do anything contrary to Himself; anything opposed to His purposes. They asked for a special favor only on the condition that the Lord should see that it was a favor. If it was not, they did not ask for it. Their prayer was answered.

The prayer of those who did not pray in the Lord's name was not answered. They asked in their own name. They asked for a specific object without conditions; they did not look beyond the event itself; they made their own wisdom the test of what was best for all. They prayed, "Let it be as I will." Such a prayer could not be offered in the Lord's name. Such a petition could not be made by one who dwelt in the Lord, and in whom the Lord's words were an abiding life and a guiding light. Their prayer was not granted. It could not be in the nature of things. If it were possible, it would involve all human affairs and the whole creation in ruin.

But some one may say, This is a mere quibble. How can two persons ask for the same favor, and the request of one be granted and the other denied, when neither of them get it? From a superficial view it does seem impossible. But let us regard the subject in the light of a familiar illustration. A wise and kind father says to his two sons, "I desire to do everything in my power for your highest good. Come to me freely; ask me any favor you please, and if, in my judgment, it be for your happiness, I will grant it." Encouraged by this promise both ask for the same thing. One of the sons says, "This favor seems to me very desirable; I think it will help me and conduce greatly to my prosperity and happiness. But I do not desire to rely upon my own judgment.  You know better than I.  If you think it is not best, I desire to abide by your judgment."  The other comes in his own name.  He pleads for it; tries to persuade his father to let him have it.  He looks only to the favor.  He judges of its value wholly by his own estimation.  He does not make any condition.

The father decides that it is not best to grant his sons' request.  He sees many ways in which it might be injurious to them.  Is it not true that, when the whole question is taken into account, the prayer of one of the sons is answered, and of the other not, though neither of them receive the particular thing asked?  The one asks for it on certain conditions, and unless those are present, he desires that his request be not granted.  Those conditions are not present, and, therefore, his request for the special favor is not granted; but as a whole it is.  The larger request, which embraced and qualified the other, is granted.  He gets what he asks, according to the conditions.  The other son made no conditions, and when the special favor was denied his whole prayer was rejected.

So it is with all the favors we ask of the Lord.  When we ask in His name the conditions are always implied.  We do not desire the Lord to grant our request, whether He sees that it is best for us or not.  We ask it if He sees that it would be good for us and for all, and can be granted without violence to the laws of the Divine Providence.  The Lord keeps His promises.  He answers every prayer offered according to the prescribed conditions, and He answers no others.  He has not promised to answer any others.  He could not answer any others; and if we could see all the bearings of giving or denying to us our requests as the Lord in His omniscience sees them, we should not desire to have the decision otherwise than He makes it.

But the Lord often answers the prayers of His people when He seems to deny them. He answers them so largely and fully; does so much better by us than we can ask or think, that the particular favor is lost sight of in the profusion of blessings. Our prayer is answered in spirit, while it is not granted in the letter. Our people prayed with united voice and heart that the life of our President might be spared to us. Why was this prayer so general and so earnest? Was it not because there was so much confidence in his ability and integrity? Was it not because of the general hope and belief that he would reform abuses, purify the currents of political thought, and improve the condition of civil service? The prayers were not so much for him personally as for the country. The intense interest in his life was excited by the hope of the use he would render the nation and the world. Are these hopes blasted? Has his influence ceased? Has he gone beyond the limits of his power to serve us?

No. His influence has not ceased. He is more alive to-day than ever before. He lives in more hearts to-day than ever before. He is a living power in more minds to-day than he would have been four years hence, after the most successful conduct of our national affairs. His principles are more widely known, and they will have more weight in forming the opinions of our people. They are beyond the reach of friend or enemy. No power can change them. No mistakes in policy; no calumny of enemies; no cunning of political artifice; no blindness of party zeal can weaken their power, or obscure their brightness. Sanctified by his martyrdom in the prime of his manhood, his memory will be cherished in the hearts of our people, and handed down from generation to generation. He lives and will continue to live. His memory will be kept green and fruitful by a tender sympathy, by a reverent admiration and a profound respect for the principles which he lived and died to maintain. Such men never die. Their principles enter into the heart of humanity and become permanent forces, which awaken affection, mould thought, and direct action. Every prayer offered for the preservation of his life has been answered.

But there is another respect in which the prayers of our people were really answered when it seemed as though they were not. Without doubt many hearts were touched with pity that he who had won his way from such low conditions, up through every grade of employment and office to the highest position in his country, if not in the world, should be hurled from it just as he was entering upon its duties and beginning to reap its rewards, and they prayed for him,—prayed that he might be spared to enjoy his well-earned success. From the point of view of earth and time, it did appear as though the cup was dashed from his lips before he could taste of the joy of success. His sun went down while it was yet day. But if it sunk below the horizon of this life, it rose above the horizon of the other into a brighter day, and better conditions for serving his country and family and attaining the true blessedness of life.

He has lost nothing personally. He is the same man, in the same noble form, the embodiment of the same principles. He is to-day what he became by the knowledge he gained and the principles which were wrought into the fabric of his spiritual nature, and became character. Not a single truth, or principle, or affection, or reward will be lost. He possesses all those qualities which excited admiration, created confidence, awakened sympathy, and won the heart. He is reaping, and will continue to reap in larger measures, his reward. He has risen to higher honors, which will be freely accorded to him with liberal hands, according to the full measure of his deserts.

Nor is he personally lost to us. He lives not only as a memory, a sentiment; not only by the truths he taught and by the influence of his example. He lives as a man. He is not removed from country, wife, and home. He is merely transferred to another province of the Lord's kingdom. He has not gone away from us. He has come nearer to the secret springs of our national life. He has been promoted from a lower to a higher and more interior plane of power, in which he can do more to guide our action and control our destiny than he could have done as our Chief Magistrate.

We are justified in the conclusion, therefore, that every sincere prayer to the Lord that He would preserve the life of our President, that he might continue to serve and bless his country, and reap the reward of his deeds, has been answered. Not, indeed, in the special way asked and hoped for; but in a wiser, fuller, and more efficient way. Shall we not be content with that? Shall we, who cannot see so much of the consequences of any act as a mole in the ground sees of the material universe, dictate to infinite wisdom in what specific form our prayers shall be answered? If a hungry man asks us for a crust, will he complain that his request is not granted when we give him a loaf? Our request may be of such a nature that it cannot be granted without our co-operation, and much labor and sorrow; and the Lord may be answering our petition while He seems to us to be denying it.

Suppose we honestly pray that our sins may be forgiven, and that we may be admitted into heaven. We may think only of the penalty, and believe that the Lord can forgive sin as a magistrate can pardon a criminal, and that we can be admitted into heaven by personal favor, as we might be to a feast. The Lord begins to answer our prayer. He suffers us to be tried and tempted that we may see our evils, see their vile and unclean nature, and put them away. Afflictions come upon us; the love of world and self is assaulted, and instead of the rest and peace of heaven, we come into infernal torment. Why is this? Has the Lord turned a deaf ear to our prayer? We asked for peace, and we find war; we prayed for rest, and we are wearied with labor and goaded by conflicting passions. If in our agony we should cry unto the Lord, "O Lord, hear me, answer me, save me!" His reply could truly be, "I do hear you, I am answering you, I am saving you." So the Lord leads us in a way we know not and could not have chosen, to the end we seek. He answers our prayer while He seems to us to reject it.

# II

# THE NATURE AND USE OF PRAYER.

*" Ask, and it shall be given you."*—Matthew vii. 7.

THE subject of prayer deeply concerns the vital interests of every human being. There is embodied in man's nature a tendency to look to the source of his life, which creates a necessity for prayer. If man had retained his original perfection it would be as natural for him to pray as it is to eat when he is hungry, to seek relief when he is in distress, or to communicate his thoughts and affections to those whom he loves. There is a sense in which every creature prays. But how prayer helps us, and in what way the good attained by it comes, remains one of those open secrets about which there is much discussion, and but little generally known.

When the opinion prevailed that the Lord acted in an arbitrary way like an irresponsible sovereign, there was no difficulty in believing that He could be moved by entreaty, and give a direct and immediate answer to any petition that pleased Him. But as men learned that the universe was governed according to immutable law, that all things are related, and that effects are dependent upon their causes, questions began to arise about the efficacy of prayer for special objects.

There are other causes of doubt, also, about the use of

27

prayer. If the Lord is a being of infinite love and desires
to confer blessings upon His children, why should He withhold them until He is asked, and even importuned? If
He will only give us what seems to Him to be best however fervently we may pray, and will give it whether we
ask Him or not, what is the use of praying?

These questions cannot be answered without some true
knowledge of our relations to the Lord. We must know
what asking is. Millions of prayers are spoken in which
no good is asked. They are merely the mechanical actions
of the memory, repeated from habit without any thought
of their meaning.

If we desire a rational answer, we must go beneath appearances, and gain a broad and comprehensive idea of
prayer. We must know something of the state of the soul
in the act of prayer, and of its attitude towards the Lord.
We must have some knowledge of the Lord's purpose in
our creation, and how His purposes and our purposes can
be united. We must see how life is received, or repelled.
In the measure and degree we can understand our true relations to the Lord we may be able to discover the essential uses of prayer. To get the subject fairly before us,
however, it may be necessary to clear away some false
ideas which have prevailed with regard to the nature and
efficacy of prayer, by considering what they are not.

1. It is not the use of prayer to give the Lord information, or to remind Him of His knowledge or promises.
He knows our sins, and how vile and false we are. He
knows how blind and ignorant and foolish we are infinitely
better than we do. He knows what hindrances lie in our
path to heaven, how poor and miserable and weary and
faint-hearted we are. He knows our spiritual condition

in all its causes and relations. Our knowledge of our-selves is as nothing compared with His. It is useful to us to confess our sins, but not for the purpose of giving the Lord information. We cannot tell Him anything He does not know infinitely better than we do, or ever can.

2. It is not the use of prayer to change His feelings or purpose towards us. If it were possible to do that, it would harm rather than help us. He has only one pur-pose with regard to every human being, and that is to do him all the good in His power. What the Lord can do for us, however, depends upon our willingness and ability to receive good from Him. If the Lord seems to be hostile to us, it is because we propose to ourselves ends of life which are selfish and worldly, and, therefore, destructive of our highest good. We identify ourselves with those purposes, and think our happiness depends upon our success in effect-ing them. The Lord opposes them because He knows how harmful they are, and we conclude that He must be hostile to us because He opposes our selfish and worldly desires. But this is a fatal fallacy, which has caused the most unjust and cruel misconceptions of the Lord's char-acter, and of His attitude towards sinful men. We regard the infinitely perfect and merciful Lord through the per-verting medium of our false principles and evil passions, and attribute to Him the distortions caused by them. But "The Lord is good to all, and His tender mercies are over all His works."

3. It is not a use of prayer to persuade the Lord by our importunities to grant our requests. There is a feeling, if not a clearly defined belief by Christians, that the Lord is somewhat reluctant to bestow blessings upon men; that He regards them with some degree of indifference, and even

aversion, and that His indifference can only be overcome, and His ear gained, by the most urgent and importunate entreaties. But this is a mistake. While the Lord regards every human being with infinite and unchanging love, He has none of the weaknesses of natural parents, who yield to the importunities of their children, and grant requests which are hurtful to them. Swedenborg says the Lord does not hear prayer in temptation on account of the end. He means that the Lord does not remove the temptation and save us from the conflict and suffering at our request while we are in it, but permits us to go through it, and sustains us in it, that we may see the evil which causes the conflict, learn its true nature, and voluntarily overcome it. The prayers of the universe could not change the purposes of infinite love, the methods of infinite wisdom, or win a more prompt and favorable regard or tender and helpful service from the Lord than He constantly accords us.

If prayer has no avail in giving information to the Omniscient, if it cannot change the purpose or methods of the Immutable, if it has no power of suasion to win a more favorable regard, and gain more efficient help in time of need from infinite love and wisdom, what is the use of it? What does it effect? Whom does it affect? How are its effects produced? Mere assertions in regard to these questions are of no special value. They may be true, or they may be false. We need some rational knowledge upon the subject; we must regard these questions from some central point of view; we must see them in the light of our relations to the Lord. Let us, therefore, consider, for a moment, what those relations are.

Man is primarily and essentially related to the Lord as a recipient of life to the source of life. He has other relations which are important, but they are secondary. This one is primary. Man is related to the Lord as the stream to the fountain, as the motions of an engine to the force which propels it. This relation is constant. "In Him we live and move and have our being." We have no inherent, underived power of any kind, spiritual, mental, or physical. All the prevalent theories of man's relation to the Lord are based on the assumption that man has some powers of his own. They may have been the gift of the Lord to the first man, but they are not constantly given to every man. They are like money or an estate bequeathed by a father to his sons. The act of transfer was a simple one, and when once completed, needed no repetition. The father dispossessed himself, and his sons came into absolute ownership and control of the inheritance.

But this is not a true idea of our relations to the Lord. Everything we possess is a constant gift, a constant transfer. It is like the gift of a fountain to a stream. If the fountain withholds its gift, the stream disappears. It is like the gift of the sun to the plant. The plant has no power stored up in itself to grow independently of the action of the sun. If the sun should withhold his light and heat, the growth of every plant would be instantly arrested.

Look at another fact. The quantity of life, or power, or substance of any kind a vessel or an organic form receives, is measured by its capacity. It is impossible to put into any vessel more than it will contain, or a substance which it cannot hold. The effect of a constant cause will vary, therefore, with the nature and capacity of the recipient form, and will always be determined by it. Let me illustrate. Take the atmosphere as one example.

When it flows into the lungs it produces a very different effect from what it does when it flows into the ear, or into the pipe of an organ. The air is a constant cause. It must act every moment or the effect ceases. The effect, also, varies with the recipient form. · Take the light as another example. The colors of all objects are caused by the light constantly acting. Put out the light and color is annihilated. The color varies, also, with the quality of the object which reflects it. In all these cases the cause is constant, but the effects are various, and the variety depends upon the recipient vessel.

Let us apply these analogies to man. The Lord is the constant cause. All life, all power to exist, to grow, to feel, think, love, act, comes from the Lord, as light and heat from the sun, by a constant inflowing. But it is variously received, according to the capacity and organic form of the mind, for the mind is an organic form in the same sense that the lungs and the heart are.

As no change in the plant increases or diminishes the heat and light of the sun, as the air remains the same whether the lungs are sound or diseased, whether the pipes of an organ are large or small, few or many, so the Lord remains the same whether men are good or evil, whether they receive life in large or small measures. The use of all means for the improvement of human character, and the increase of human happiness, must, therefore, consist in its effect upon men. If we desire to improve the quality of a plant we do it by better culture, not by changing the quality of the sun; if we desire to get richer harmonies from an organ, we change its pipes and not the air. So we can only remove human imperfections, improve the quality of human character, and gain larger measures of human happiness by acting upon man himself. All changes must be made in the recipients of life, none in the life itself. It is from this central, organic, substantial, and constant relation of man to the Lord that we can discover the use of prayer, and see whom it helps, and how it renders its service. Let us consider the subject from this point of view.

Prayer is asking. Can you not think of any other kind of asking than with the lips? The eye can ask, the face can ask, the hands can ask, the whole body can ask. A dumb man can ask, a dog can ask, even a plant can ask. The postures of the body and vocal utterance only express the real prayer within. Everything that receives asks, and it only receives what it asks, and it does receive what it asks. Every one that asketh receiveth. Asking is not merely making known a want, it is an effort to gain the means of supplying it. But what a man is will determine his prayer and the answer.

Prayer is converse with the Lord. Take the lowest and most external form of it. It is an expression of some thought or affection, if it is not wholly mechanical. In this act we do think of the Lord. We turn, for the moment at least, to Him. There is some acknowledgment of Him. Is there no use in that? Take the prayer of a little child, for example, who has only the most natural conceptions of the Lord. Is it not of some use to the child to turn its thoughts to a being above itself? Does it not turn its face and set its tender feet in the right direction? Does it not have some effect in making its nature, while it is soft and yielding, pliant to the sweet attractions of the Divine love? The influence may be very slight, it may be no more than a tendency; but it must

3

have some effect, and that effect must be useful. It must tend to place the child in a state to receive more and richer blessings from the Lord.

Is there no relief and no help in expressing our thoughts and affections to others? We go to dear friends and tell them our difficulties, trials, wants, sorrows; not, it may be, with any expectation of getting direct help from them. We unburden our souls. What does that mean,— unburden? It means to cast off our burden. Does it not lighten the weight a little? Even if our friends cannot remove it, we get strength from their sympathy to support it. How many sorrowing souls would have given up in despair, their life crushed out of them, if it had not been for the sympathy and encouragement of friends? If we find such help from converse with our fellow-men, shall we get none from the Lord when we " pour out our souls" to Him?

Here it is important to observe that the use does not consist in giving information, even to our friends, much less to the Lord. The use consists in its effect upon us. It loosens the hold of sorrow upon us; it lifts up the burden and throws it from our shoulders. It brings us into a state in which the Lord in some measure can help us.

All genuine prayer is attended with humiliation. It has a tendency to humble us, and it does it in the degree that we have any true feeling and conception of our condition and needs. As the true light begins to shine into our understandings and hearts, it reveals the darkness which prevails there. It shows our ignorance, our stupidity, our deformities, our enmities, and impurities, and no man or woman can see their own evils and falsities without some degree of shame and humiliation. The more clearly we see them in heavenly light the deeper must be our self-abasement. Our alienation from the Lord, and our spiritual deformities are too great for utterance. We feel more like putting our " hands upon our mouths, and our mouths in the dust." Instead of justifying ourselves, we cannot lift our eyes to heaven. We can only smite upon our breast and cry, " God be merciful to me a sinner." We come as prodigals, and our prayer is, " I am no longer worthy to be called thy son, make me as one of thy hired servants."

This is a state of surrender to the Lord. So far as we come into it, we yield ourselves to His guidance and power. We cease to dictate to Him; we cease to claim anything for ourselves; we give up our wills and under-standings to be governed and moulded by the Divine Wisdom. In this denial of our own self-derived intelligence, and surrender of ourselves to the Lord, consists the use of humiliation. The Lord has no desire to see us pros-trate and terrified like slaves before Him. On the con-trary, He desires to make us sons, and not slaves or hired servants. He desires to have us stand upon our feet and act like free men. Humiliation is the abasement of the natural man; it is putting the sensual desires and passions under our feet; it is the denial of our love of self and the world, and abhorrence of error and sin. So far as we do that we come into a state in which the Lord can help us; we remove the obstacles to the reception of those forces which give us life. Humiliation is really the effect of some true knowledge and love of the Lord; it is due to heavenly principles and powers. They drive out the vile, disorderly, corrupt inhabitants of our mental house, and open the door for the Lord to come in and " sup with us and we with Him."

Prayer has a tendency to cause this humiliation. It brings us face to face with the Lord on the one hand and our own corrupt natures on the other. We see the contrast, and in the degree we see it we must abhor the evil, we must be humbled at the thought that we have loved and cherished and become the embodiment of principles which are repugnant to everything which is good and true. So prayer tends to bring us into such relations to the Lord that He can forgive our sins, wash us and make us clean, and remove all obstacles to the full possession of our souls.

Prayer is lifting up the eyes and turning the heart to the Lord. The natural plane of our natures, in which resides our consciousness, and which is the theatre of our acquired and habitual life, has become inverted. It has been turned away from heaven and the Lord, and bent downward to the earth; it has been closed to the direct and orderly influx of Divine, sanctifying, and living forces, and opened to the world. The mind is an organized form, and is subject to all the laws of organization. When I speak of it as inverted, bent from its original uprightness, its vessels closed to the inflowing of the pure water of life, and opened to the standing pools and polluted streams of sensual and worldly influences, I do not use a figure. I utter a fact. Prayer is an effort to restore it to its original order; to lift it up from the earth; to open its closed and withered vessels to the vivifying power of the Holy Spirit. This is a slow and painful process. It can only be gradually effected, especially when the natural mind has become hard and fixed by habit. It must be bent, not broken. We could not bear the strain of a sudden conversion.

Is there no use in this effort? If we can turn our thoughts towards the Lord and raise them from the earth a little, is there no use in that? If we can catch a glimpse of the heavenly light; if we can inhale a vivifying breath of the heavenly atmosphere; if we can even get a taste of the pure water of the river of life; if we can get a drop of its water on our parched tongues to cool the fever of earthly passions even for a moment, is there no saving efficacy, no gain in that?

If we consider the source of the influence which leads us to the closet and bends our knees in prayer, we may see some possibility of its use. The prayer is due to Divine influence. The moving cause in the soul is the Divine life working there in its secret closets, brooding over the chaos of worldly affections struggling through the dense clouds of sensual illusions. The prayer we voice comes from the Lord, and is given to us to make our own. It is His voice speaking with our lips. He teaches us how to pray, and we cannot pray without His teaching. How faint the voice from within is! It is almost drowned in the clamors of our worldly passions. It may come from the fading memories of childhood; it may seem to be an echo from a mother's influence; it may seem to come from without; but it is the Divine love calling to us; it is the power of His Spirit working in us, to mould our distorted natures into the Divine likeness; it is the attraction of His power lifting us up and bending us towards Him. Every true prayer voices the working of the Lord in us. Do we say "Our Father" with any filial affection, we co-operate with the Lord in making Him more fully our father. Do we implore with any sincerity, "Forgive us our debts," we express what He is trying to do, and by the expression help Him in His work. Do we pray, "Thy kingdom come," with an honest desire. It is coming. We could not ask it if it were not, and by asking we hasten its coming. Prayer is a revelation; it shows what the Lord is doing, or trying to do in us and for us. Prayer welcomes His coming, prepares a place to lay His Divine head, and helps Him in His work of saving and blessing us.

Prayer is communion with the Lord. This is something more than speech. It may exist without it. Communion is exchange of gifts; it is the sharing of a common blessing; it is the blending of the life of one being with another while each preserves its distinct personality. This is the relation of the branch and the vine. This is what our Lord means when He says, "Abide in me, and I in you." "If ye abide in me and my words abide in you, ye shall ask what ye will, and it shall be done unto you." There is an actual opening of the inmost vessels of the affections to the Divine forces which give us life. Those forces, which are in reality the substances of which our spiritual bodies are woven, are received and appropriated; they are taken up and become a part of our being, as the substances of which the blood is composed are taken up by the various organs of the body and become a part of them. This communion is eating the Lord's flesh and drinking His blood by which we have eternal life. The Divine life is communicated to us. It penetrates our life, softens the hardness of our spiritual natures; imbues them with some of its own qualities; finites in them some of its infinite perfections; tends to impart its motions and order to their activities, and to bring their forms and movements into voluntary accord with its infinite harmonies. So far as we yield to the brooding warmth of these influent Divine forces, we receive refreshment and vigor from them. They vitalize our affections and clarify our understandings, and we carry this renewal of our strength into all our duties and relations of life. We get help in resisting evil and power to overcome in temptation; our understanding becomes so luminous and true that we can see the path which leads to eternal life through all the labyrinths of worldly interests and the illusions of sensual desires. The Lord has gained such a powerful hold upon us that He can raise us up by the attractions of His love and draw us towards Himself, as the magnet separates the particles of iron from the sand and draws them to its own embrace.

This communion may come to our consciousness as a calm, inward joy, as peace and rest. But the effect may not be discernible immediately. These Divine forces, received when we open our hearts to the Lord in sincere prayer, may require many years before they can speak loud enough to be heard amid the discords and clamors of worldly passions; before they can soften the hardness of our natures sufficiently to make an impression upon them which can be felt. But every sincere prayer is a yielding to them; gives them a little advantage; and the ground they gain they hold. As they advance in bringing our natures into harmony with the Divine nature, the seasons of peace and rest become more frequent and of longer continuance, the rest is more complete, and the peace sinks into blessedness. This is the rest and peace of heaven. It comes by communion with the Lord. We taste, and we do see that the Lord is good. We experience the great peace which those enjoy who love the law of the Lord. It is a rest, and a peace, and a joy, which fills the soul when it comes into the harmonies of the Divine order.

If prayer puts us into the proper attitude to receive

such influences, to obtain such help in our conflicts with evil, and opens the door of entrance into such pure and endless blessings, is it not a most powerful means of our regeneration, and of inestimable use in gaining heaven? It prepares the way and leads to the end for which all other things are given us. In answering the prayer that our sins may be forgiven, and that we may become one with the Lord, does He not answer all prayers?

These are the real uses of prayer. They comprehend all particulars. They accord with the Lord's purpose in our creation. Their real effect is not upon the Lord, but upon ourselves. They tend to put us into such relations to the Lord that He can do more for us than He could if we did not pray. They may cause such a change in us that those around us, both on the spiritual and the natural side of life, can help us. The Lord provides everything possible for our highest good. But what He can do for us depends upon our capacity of receiving good from Him. He cannot do for the infant just born so much as He can for the youth. He cannot give to the youth the affections and thoughts and physical strength of an adult man. He cannot give to a rock the virtues and graces, the transcendent beauty and glowing love of an angel. He cannot give to a false, perverted, corrupt nature the sweetness and purity, the wisdom, joy, and peace which He can bestow upon those who bear His own image and likeness. Any act or attainment by man which removes the obstacles to the reception of the Divine life, or enlarges his capacities, is of great use to him.

As man is the only one who requires to be changed, it is not difficult to see that it may be far more useful to man that his prayers should be answered through his instrumentality than directly without it. The answer may be more effective and lasting. Take a pestilence as an example. The belief was once general that plagues and cholera were scourges sent by the Lord in anger as a punishment for man's sins, and prayers were offered up in all churches that they might be stayed by a direct interposition of almighty power. Suppose such prayers could have been, and had been answered. It would have caused a thousandfold more suffering and death than the pestilence. It would have prevented men from looking for the natural causes of disease, and removing them. Thousands of lives are gradually destroyed by filth and the violation of the laws of health to one which is swept away by pestilence. Carry out the principle into all human relations, and it would take away from man all prudence, all foresight, all motives to obtain knowledge, all stimulus to human effort. If the Lord will stay a pestilence at the request of men, why should he not heal all diseases? or prevent them in the beginning? If He will send rain, moved by the prayers of Christians, why will He not regulate the seasons with special reference to every location and every want? Why will He not keep all men in perfect health, and supply all human needs and desires without any effort or thought on man's part? Why will He not correct all wrong, save from all suffering, however unwise and sinful men may act?

The answer is evident. If the Lord made such special provisions for every human want, and protected man from the consequences of ignorance, error, and sin, He would destroy all the pleasures of activity, all the rewards of wise conduct. He would reduce every man to the same level, and all to the condition of the brute.

Our prayers and the Lord's method of answering them are a part of this universal method of the Divine order. He incites us to ask that we may come into a state to receive an answer. But He answers us through our own efforts, when those efforts are of such a nature that He can grant our request by means of them. Millions of prayers are offered every day for the salvation of men. The Lord is answering them as fast and as fully as He can. We pray that the " Lord's will may be done on the earth as it is in heaven." It is useful to us to make the prayer, because if we offer it in sincerity, it will lead us to do what we can to aid in the establishment of the Lord's kingdom upon the earth. He is answering the prayer as fast as possible; but He can only do it by means of the men and women who constitute that kingdom.

From these considerations we conclude that the use of prayer consists in awakening our own interests in the object of our petition, in calling forth our efforts to obtain it, and in bringing us into such orderly and intimate relations with the Lord, who is the source of all power and life, that He can work through us and bless us in granting our requests.

# III.

## HYPOCRITICAL AND VAIN PRAYER.

---

*"And when thou prayest, thou shalt not be as the hypocrites are : for they love to pray standing in the synagogues and in the corners of the streets, that they may be seen of men. Verily I say unto you They have their reward.*

*" But when ye pray, use not vain repetitions as the heathen do : for they think that they will be heard for their much speaking.*

*" Be not ye therefore like unto them : for your Father knoweth what things ye have need of, before ye ask Him."*
—Matthew vi. 5, 7, 8.

THE Lord not only bestows upon us every good which we possess, but He instructs us how to get it, how to use it, how to increase it, and how to avoid the obstacles which hinder its reception and enjoyment and cause us to miss the true ends of life. As man is in evil and falsity by nature, the first essential truth for him to learn is, what to avoid. When we are going in the wrong direction, we must discover our error and change our course before we can reach the goal we seek. The Lord, therefore, begins His instruction concerning alms, prayer, and fasting by telling us what we must avoid. Eight of the ten commandments are prohibitory. In the work of regeneration and the formation of a spiritual and heavenly mind, thou shalt not must always precede thou shalt.

In considering the subject of prayer let us follow the same order, and first learn how we must not pray. It will be a great help to us to understand the false forms and evil motives of prayer. It will free the subject from misconceptions, and false methods, and forms, and simplify it in every respect. When we know what to avoid we can easily learn what to do. There is no part of religious worship, of private or of public devotion, which is more misunderstood than prayer. Its nature is not generally known; there are many misconceptions of its use, and of the manner in which that use is effected. Let us try to discover what these false notions are; then we shall be able to learn how to pray, for what to pray, and what good we may hope to gain by prayer.

First, our Lord instructs us with regard to the motives of prayer. We must not pray from any selfish or worldly motive. "When thou prayest, thou shalt not be as the hypocrites:" they pray "to be seen of men." What is a hypocrite? A hypocrite is one who feigns to be what he is not; he assumes a character which he does not possess. He acts from different motives from those which he professes. When he pretends to worship God, he is worshipping himself. When he appears to be seeking the Divine favor, he is looking for the favor of men. He is seeking to gain credit for a love and a regard for the Lord which he does not possess. Hypocrisy has many forms and degrees of baseness, but a religious hypocrite is the vilest and most contemptible of all. He assumes the highest and purest virtues for the lowest ends ; he clothes himself with the spotless garments of heaven to cover the deformities and malignities of hell. He comes to his Divine Master in the character of a devoted and loving disciple, but betrays Him with a kiss. But our Lord has given us some of his characteristics and methods which, when analyzed and unfolded in spiritual light, will exhibit his animus and genuine nature in true colors, and reveal the wickedness and the uselessness of vain repetitions and a merely formal devotion.

Hypocrites *love* to pray. No men are more devout in attitude, deferential in tone, earnest in manner, and punctilious in the performance of their devotions. They love to do it. It gives them the odor of sanctity ; it gratifies their vanity ; it lulls their consciences to sleep ; it makes them conspicuous in the public eye ; it tends to gain the favor of men. See what a devout and holy man ! the multitude will exclaim. But this love is not the love of God or of man. It is the love of themselves. They pretend to be worshipping the Lord, but in reality they are adoring themselves. They give homage to the Lord with their lips, but they are claiming it for themselves in their thoughts. They ask favors of the Lord in form, while in their intentions they are seeking them from men. The apparent purpose of their prayers is to gain a hearing and favorable notice from the Lord, their real end is to be seen of men. What mockery must such a prayer be ! To stand up conspicuously in an assembly of men and with the lips offer supplications to our heavenly Father, while we are thinking only of the praise of men ! With what infinite pity must the Lord regard the mere semblance of man who is guilty of such folly and wickedness. Whatever may be the success in deceiving men, and gaining a momentary reputation for a sanctity which they do not possess, must not the inevitable and final result be a greater damnation?

Hypocrites love to pray " standing in the synagogues." The natural meaning and the reason for selecting a public and conspicuous place for their prayers is evident when we know what favor they hope to gain by them. But these words have a spiritual and consequently a universal meaning. Every human being who has any religion, or who pretends to possess any, has a synagogue in his own mind, in which he offers his prayers and performs his devotions. These words therefore apply to us as well as to the Pharisees who lived in Jerusalem when our Lord trod its streets with weary feet, and taught in the synagogues of the Jews with a wisdom and power which filled the dead formalists with amazement.

A synagogue was a house devoted to worship and religious instruction. By a very common law of the human mind the material instrument becomes a symbol of the use to which it is applied. We see an example of this law in the common use of the word church. Its material meaning is the building in which the men and women who constitute the church assemble. The people are the real church; but they are only so far a church as they have become the embodiment and living forms of the doctrines which make those who acknowledge and live according to them a church. A synagogue, then, in its universal and genuine meaning, is the doctrine which men believe. To stand and pray in them is to pray according to the doctrines of religion they have learned and accepted. There-

fore it is that we all have our synagogue where we offer
our prayers. Standing at the corners of the streets has
the same general meaning, only a more external and special
one. A city as well as a synagogue represents doctrine,
and a street is some special truth which, with others, com-
poses the doctrine. A corner is formed by the intersection
of the streets, and represents their connection with one
another. This conjunction affords the means of seeing and
of being seen in material streets. In spiritual streets, which
are the paths our thoughts and affections pursue to the
attainment of their ends, they show the relations and con-
firmations of the various truths which taken together constitute our doctrine. Therefore corners denote firmness.
As they bind together the sides of a building and give
firmness and stability to it, so they are the points where
truth is joined to truth in logical order, and give solidity
and strength to the whole system of faith. They are also
centres towards which various truths converge, and from
which those who accept them can see and be seen. To pray
standing in the corners of the streets, represents a state of
mind in which we act according to principles which we
have adopted from various considerations. We take our
mental position where truths or falsities converge and confirm one another, where their relations can be seen, and by
means of which the love of self and the world can win
over the understanding to its delusions.

Doctrine teaches us whom to address, how to pray, and
what to pray for, because doctrine teaches us concerning
the Lord, our own natures, and our relations to Him.
Every one must, therefore, pray in the synagogue or in the
corners of the streets in his own mind. He must do it in
a good sense, even when he enters his closet and shuts the

door. But hypocrites pray only from doctrine or faith alone, and every prayer offered from truth or doctrine alone is more or less hypocritical. There are various forms and degrees of such prayer, which it may be well to consider:

1. Intellectual prayer. Prayer consists essentially in *asking*. It is a sincere, earnest desire for some good, or what seems to the suppliant to be good. It is a turning of the soul to the Lord, as the plant turns to the sun. It is an opening of the affections to the reception of the Divine Love. It can be made without words, without distinct thought even. A true prayer is before thought, before speech. Thought is only the form of it; speech is only the expression of it. A petition made from doctrine alone, from a merely intellectual conception of the Divine nature and our relations to the Lord, lacks the essential elements of prayer. It is merely the form of it, the clothing of it put on for the occasion. The intellect cannot pray; it cannot ask. Asking is not its office. Its business consists in seeing, in collecting materials to give body and form and permanent existence to the affections. Such is the nature of the human mind that the form can exist without any life in it.

All prayer from doctrine or from truth alone is hypocritical. It is not what it appears to be. There may be appropriate ascriptions of praise to the Lord, but no praise is given to Him. There may be the most humble confession of sin in words, but no sins are confessed. There is no humiliation of heart, no shame for sins committed, no loathing of a vile, corrupt nature, no sorrow because we have sinned against infinite love and wisdom. On the contrary, the hypocrite is proud of his verbal humility.

Men will think well of him, because he pretends to think so meanly of himself. The form of the prayer may be appropriate to the occasion, beautiful and eloquent; but it is addressed to the audience and not to the Lord. We sometimes hear it said of ministers and others that they are gifted in prayer. It is probable that from a human and merely intellectual point of view the praise is worthily bestowed, and that the subjects of it think so too. But viewed from the Lord, no prayer may have been offered to Him. If it was made to be eloquent, if the suppliant was well pleased with it, it was offered standing in the synagogue, or in the corners of the streets to be seen of men.

Prayer to the Lord must have the Lord, not self nor man, in view. It must go to the point. There must be some special favor desired, and that must be sought with simplicity and directness. Earnestness and sincerity do not seek for elegant phrases; they do not deal in vague generalities. Elegant phrasing and a skilful play of words are contrary to its nature. The Lord is not moved by eloquent verbiage, especially when He does not enter into the thought of the supplicant. If He were not infinitely merciful and kind, He might be moved to indignation by such hypocrisy.

Perhaps we can more fully appreciate the essential quality of a merely doctrinal prayer, however beautiful in form it may be, by regarding it from the relations of parent to child. Suppose a child who had been disobedient and desired forgiveness, or who sought a favor, should address his father in the language and style of many of the prayers we read in books of devotion and hear in public worship. He begins with ascriptions of praise; tells his father how kind and wise and good he is; ex-

4

presses his astonishment that he has borne with him
as long as he has ; prays that he will forgive him and his
brothers and sisters, and all the bad little boys and girls in
the whole world and make them obedient and good, and
finally bestow all his property upon them and make them
happy. Suppose a prayer to this effect was written out
or committed to memory and repeated every morning and
evening, repeated with roving eyes and wandering thoughts,
or with an air of conceit and an evident regard for its
effect upon others, could any quality be found in such
a devotional exercise to commend? Would it indicate
any love for the father, any sorrow for disobedience?
Would there be any heart, any sincerity, in it? Does
the child really ask anything? What would you, as a
father or mother, think of such a child, especially if he
went on in the same course of disobedience and praying
from week to week and year to year? Such a practice
could not appear otherwise than absurd, hypocritical, and
wicked. Is not that what multitudes of professed Christians are constantly doing? They ask nothing, they confess nothing, they desire nothing which the words they
use imply. They stand in a false attitude before the Lord
and men. " When ye pray be not as the hypocrites."

2. Prayer from doctrine, or faith alone, becomes formal
and mechanical and essentially hypocritical, though there
may not be any conscious desire " to be seen of men."
It is hypocritical because there is no meaning in it. We
continue to pray because we have formed a habit of praying, or because others pray. Neither the affection nor
the thoughts rise to the Lord. No honor is ascribed to
Him, no sins are confessed to Him, no help is asked from
Him. There is no spiritual, and but little, if any, natural,

life in this formal devotion. If the words could have been uttered by a machine there would have been just as much prayer in them. They are repeated by machines.

But even in this mechanical and soulless prayer there is some regard for the opinion of men. Multitudes go to the house of prayer to see and to be seen, not to worship the Lord, or to learn anything concerning their obligations to Him, and how they may fulfil them. They go because their acquaintances go; they go because it is respectable to do so. They read and respond, or sit in respectful silence, because it is the fashion, because it is the right and proper thing to do. It has the appearance of being devout; it saves them from the suspicion of unbelief or of indifference to religion. It is also often a passport by which they gain entrance into coveted social circles, or a means of securing financial favors, or influences favorable to professional success. In some way they desire to be seen of men rather than to be seen of the Lord and gain heavenly blessings from Him.

3. There is a prevalent opinion that there is some efficacy in prayer itself to procure the Divine favor; that prayer commends us to the Lord, and induces Him to bestow blessings upon us which He would otherwise withhold. According to this idea, when we have gone through with the routine of our devotions, we have done our duty; we have shown our respect for the Lord; we have given Him the tribute of our praise; we have confessed our sins, and disposed Him to forgive us. We have satisfied our consciences, and we can rest with some degree of gratification and peace. We may not have had a motion of gratitude in our hearts for favors received; there may not have been a pang of sorrow, or a sense of shame for

an idle, frivolous, and evil life ; there may not have been an aspiration for meekness, humility, purity, and a genuine spiritual character. But we have repeated the prescribed prayers in a perfunctory way ; we have complied with the prescribed forms; and the Lord must regard us with some degree of favor.

Herein lies the danger of a ritualistic form of worship, whether public or private. Whatever we do habitually, we are in danger of doing without thought or affection. We act mechanically.. There is but little room for doubt that much of our public worship is of this character. It can be seen in the listless manner of the worshippers, in the roving eye, in the automatical way in which the prayers and responses are repeated. Words, the most weighty and solemn the lips ever utter, do not express a thought or embody an affection. If we addressed the same words in such an indifferent manner to a human being, we should at once be regarded as hypocrites. And yet there is a feeling of self-satisfaction in such formal worship, as though we had performed some worthy service.

On the other hand, it is supposed by many that the efficacy of prayer depends upon natural fervor and vociferation. Consequently those who are of this opinion work themselves up into an artificial excitement. They pray loud and long in forced and unnatural tones. They agonize, or try to do it ; they beseech and implore for favors which, at heart, they do not want. They wrestle with the Lord, as they suppose, like Jacob. But there is no agony in their hearts ; there is no burning love of the Lord or the neighbor exalting and intensifying their desires. The Lord is not so remote or deaf that He cannot hear. He is not reluctant to forgive our sins and bestow the blessings of His love and wisdom upon us. This forced fervor and apparent earnestness is hypocritical. It does not flow from the heart. Let us heed the Lord's words, " When thou prayest, thou shalt not be as the hypocrites."

4. Our Lord also warns us against multiplying words in our prayers. " But when ye pray, use not vain repetitions, as the heathen do: for they think they shall be heard for their much speaking. Be ye not therefore like unto them: for your Father knoweth what things ye have need of before ye ask Him." In these words our Lord teaches us that the effect of praying is not in the volume of it, nor in the repetition of our requests. The practice of repeating many prayers may not be hypocritical, but it is the result of a total misconception of the Lord's character and of His relations to men. There is no necessity of telling Him what He knows for the purpose of giving Him information. He understands our condition infinitely better than we do. There is no necessity for importunity. He is not like a weak or selfish earthly parent who must be persuaded to grant a favor. He is more willing to give the richest blessings than we are to receive them. He does not need to be won over to regard us with favor and to forgive our sins by incessant pleading. He is in the constant effort to forgive us. No change is required in Him.

If we had a true idea of the Lord and knew how He regards every human being, the uselessness and folly of using " vain repetitions" and of " much speaking" would appear in the most convincing light. We should see that it would be impossible for any man or woman with such knowledge to pray as multitudes do at the present day. How can we implore the Lord to regard us with favor when we know that He loves us with an infinite and unchanging affection? How can we beseech Him in varied phrase to forgive our sins, when we know that there is nothing in the universe He so ardently desires? How can we ask the Father to have mercy upon us, and then turn to the Son and beg Him to have mercy upon us, and then beseech the Holy Spirit to have mercy upon us, when we know that there is but one Divine Being? It is as absurd as it would be for a child to ask her father's heart to grant her a favor, and then to beseech his head to have mercy, and end by imploring his power or life to grant the request. A child has too much sense to do this. How could we ask the Father to grant us a favor for the sake of His Son? How could we ask the Son to intercede for us with the Father, when there is only one Divine Being in existence; when in Jesus Christ "dwells the fulness of the Godhead bodily"? When we see Him we see the Father; when we address Him we address the Father, as we see the man in his material body and address him in it. When we worship Him we adore the only proper object of worship. There is no access to the Father but by the Son, as there is no access to a man's affections but by his body and intellectual faculties. But even if there were three Divine Persons in the Trinity, what reason, propriety, or sense can there be in asking one Divine Person to do a favor for the sake of another, when each one must be equally desirous of conferring the blessing? Can there be any vainer repetitions than appealing to one and then to another, and then to another, when by the verbal confession of all Christians there can be only one God?

It is "a vain repetition" to ply the Lord with motives

or reasons for granting the favors we ask. In the famous Litany which is repeated every week in all Christian lands, the Good Lord is implored to deliver us, " by the mystery of His holy Incarnation, by His holy nativity and circumcision ; by His Baptism, Fasting, and Temptation ; by His Agony and Bloody Sweat; by His Cross and Passion ; by His Precious Death and Burial ; by His glorious Resurrection and Ascension ; and by the coming of the Holy Ghost." These, it would seem if they have any meaning, are presented as motives by the suppliant to excite the Divine compassion and secure a favorable hearing. The ground for this enumeration of incidents in the life and death of our Lord, must be that they will have a cumulative effect upon Him ; that He will be more moved, and disposed to grant deliverance from evils mentioned by being reminded of what He has suffered and done for us. This is the motive of the whole Litany. The Father, Son, and Holy Spirit are implored separately and then together, and many particulars are enumerated, some of which, at least, are founded upon total misconception of the nature of the Lord, of our relations to Him, and of what is essential to our salvation from sin and eternal happiness.

5. Our Lord warns us against the frequent repetition of the same prayer. In some rituals His own prayer is repeated several times, and in a rapid mechanical manner clearly indicating that the words do not express any desire of the hearts of those who use them. If there is any motive for such repetition, it must be the belief that there is more efficacy in repeating a prayer twice than once, and that whatever good is gained by it comes as a reward for repeating it, and not in answer to any sincere desire of the heart. In one branch of the Christian Church it is cus-

tomary to keep an account of the number of times certain prayers are repeated, and the supposition is that the greater the number the greater the virtue. They think they will be heard for their "much speaking."

This is the opinion and practice, our Lord says, of the heathen or Gentiles. The Jewish nation represented the Church. All other nations they called heathen or Gentiles. The Gentiles, therefore, represent those who do not belong to the Church. They may be external members of it, but if the principles and life of heaven are not in them, they are not really members of it; they are Gentiles in principle and practice; they are heathen. These vain repetitions, therefore, and the idea that those who make them will be heard for their much speaking, are heathenish. Those who practice them are ignorant of the true principles of Christianity. They are essentially idolaters, and their prayers and worship are based upon the same principles as those who worship idols,—the principle that the Being whom they worship is hostile to them and needs propitiating: that He regards His worshippers as servants, and is pleased with servility and adulation; that He punishes those who neglect Him, and bestows His favors upon those who are assiduous in their devotions; that He loves to see the people prostrate before Him, and to hear His own praise and glory sounded from their lips; that He is reluctant to bless, easily irritated by neglect, and enraged by opposition.

A great number of the prayers offered in our churches to-day are the outbirth and expression of this idea of the Lord, of the service He exacts of men, and the way to secure His favor. According to this idea, prayer is not the communion of a loving child with a revered and beloved parent; it is not an outpouring of gratitude for favors constantly received; it is not ascriptions of praise from a reverent and adoring heart; it is not the confession of sin from sincere penitence; it is not a petition for help to overcome evils which are clearly seen and abhorred; it is not an aspiration of the soul for a higher, purer, sweeter, nobler life. If it were, the petitions could not be multiplied and wordy, and repeated in a cold, mechanical manner. Sincere, deep, and earnest feeling does not express itself in that manner. A deep and loathing sense of sin cannot reiterate in measured tones, in varied and precise form, a petition for mercy. It is more likely to be mute or an inarticulate cry, or with the eyes bent to the earth for shame, the appeal of the publican, while smiting upon his breast, an appeal wrung from a breaking heart, " God be merciful to me a sinner."

There is no warrant in reason, in the nature of man, or of the Lord for the roundabout indefinite praying for all sorts and conditions of men to be saved from evils and calamities which do not threaten us, for blessings which we do not desire, for graces which we will not receive, for the accomplishment of objects to effect which we will not lift a finger. We never ask men for grace or favor in this way. There are no such examples of prayer in the Sacred Scriptures. When our Lord was upon the earth, and men came for favors, they had something definite to ask. Blind Bartimeus knew what he wanted, and to the question, " What wouldst thou that I should do unto thee?" his prompt and earnest cry was, " Lord, that my eyes may be opened." Jairus knew what he wanted. He knew that his beloved daughter, the light of his house and the joy of his heart, was dying. When he saw the Lord he fell at His feet and besought Him greatly, saying, "**My** little daughter lieth at the point of death; come and lay thy hands upon her that she may be healed, and she shall live." There was nothing hypocritical in their prayers. They did not pray to be seen of men. They had no formal and stereotyped and indefinite request to make. They used no "vain repetitions;" they were not heard for their "much speaking." It was their sincerity and confidence in the Lord which brought them into such relations to Him that His Divine power could take effect upon them.

This subject is one of present, personal application to us. Our Lord says to each one of us to-day, "When thou prayest, thou shall not be as the hypocrites." "When ye pray, use not vain repetitions." Those who pray in these ways against which our Lord warns us, have their reward. The hypocrite is seen of men, and for a brief space gains a reputation from those who only see him standing in the synagogue, or at the corners of the streets, for sanctity and devotion. Those who use vain repetitions get their reward. But with both classes it is a poor and transitory one. It comes from men who cannot assuage our sorrows, save from death, or raise us up into everlasting life. "When ye pray be not like the hypocrites," the formalists, the ignorant and misguided Gentiles, and think not that He who looks only upon the heart, and can answer only those prayers which come from the heart, can be influenced by lip service or "vain repetitions."

# IV

# CONDITIONS AND NATURE OF GENUINE PRAYER.

———————

"*But when thou prayest, enter into thy closet, and when thou hast shut thy door, pray to thy Father which is in secret; and thy Father which seeth in secret shall reward thee openly.*"—Matthew vi. 6.

IN these words the Lord, our infinitely wise teacher and unchanging friend, instructs us concerning the conditions and nature of sincere, genuine, effective prayer. He teaches us where we must offer it, what precautions we must use to guard against the disturbance of our thoughts and affections while we are engaged in it, and to whom we must direct it. He tells us where to find our Heavenly Father, how to get access to Him, and encourages us to look into the infinite secrets of the Divine love and wisdom, with the assurance that the Lord will reward us openly for every step we take in the knowledge of Divine truth, and the life of the Divine love.

As the Lord is infinitely wise, this instruction must be given in an infinitely wise way; it must be adapted to all

states of progress from the first steps of spiritual disciple-
ship to the wisdom of the highest angels. It must be
adapted to all times and adequate to all wants. A part of
the natural directions are simple and easily understood. A
child knows what it is to enter a closet and shut the door
and pray to the Father, but the wisest may not fully comprehend what is meant by the Father in secret, by His
seeing in secret, and how He will reward us openly.
When we penetrate beneath the surface of the natural
meaning, we come into the wide realm of causes. We
pass out of the shadows and illusions of the material
world into the light of the permanent and the real.
Taking the doctrines of spiritual truth for our guide and
light, let us see to what secret treasures of love and wisdom they will lead us, and what rewards they will openly
reveal to us.

1. First let us find the closet we are directed to enter.
The word translated closet means an inner chamber, or
a treasury where the most precious things are kept. It is
the most retired and secret room in the house, where its
occupants are hidden from outward observation. Such a
closet is to a house as the heart, or the will and the affections, are to the human mind. The heart is the treasury
of the soul. There are deposited all our most precious
treasures; there are the ends and motives of life which
are the standards by which we measure all values,—" out
of the heart are the issues of life." There we have laid
up our treasures of money and lands, of knowledge and
position. There are all whom we love. Enter and look
around. You will see their faces, though some may be in
other lands and some in other worlds. There, also, and
only there can we find the Lord. The kingdom of God

is within us. The Lord can only dwell in His own kingdom, in the love and wisdom which are akin to His own nature and which are from Himself. The closet into which we are directed to enter is formed by our inmost affections, the primary ends of life. There our Heavenly Father dwells in secret.

2. How do we enter that inner, secret chamber of the soul? By a severe scrutiny of the real ends we seek in prayer. The hypocrite does not enter the closet; he stands in the synagogue or in the corners of the streets. He is not seeking the Father in secret, but the popular ear without. Those who pray in a merely formal and mechanical manner do not pass into the inner chamber of the soul; they stand without in the memory or doctrine alone, and pray to empty space. Those only enter the closet who go down to the inmost recesses of their motives; who form some distinct idea of what they desire; of the august and glorious Being whom they have come to meet, and whose forgiveness and blessing they desire to implore. Search the motives which lead you to pray. When you enter the closet take the Divine truth with you as a light. Let it reveal your worldly and selfish affections; let it throw its pure and searching light into every corner and hiding-place of your most hidden motives. In thought, guided by the light of Divine truth, we enter the closet.

3. "And when thou hast shut thy door." What door? The door of entrance into the closet, the door which separates the inmost recesses of the soul from the more external principles of our nature. Truth is a door because it gives us access to the principles, laws, and order of the causes and substances to which it relates. Love is a door which admits us into the secret and most exquisite bless-

ings of life. Every false principle and evil desire is a door which opens into the realms of darkness, sorrow, and death. To enter the chamber and shut the door is directly contrary to the practice of the hypocrite, or of those who think they will be heard for their much speaking. It consists in acting without regard to the opinions, the censure, or the applause of men. The hypocrite prays to be seen of men: the true Christian to be seen of the Lord. We are naturally in evils and false principles which lead us to look outwardly to men and to ourselves for the gratification of our selfish and worldly desires. These desires will struggle to keep possession of our thoughts and affections, and when we shut the door against them they will clamor for admission. The door is formed by truths which reveal their true character, and we must be faithful and resolute in shutting it.

4. How can we shut this door? Evidently by ceasing to think falsely and to act wickedly. A truth or falsity is shut when we cease to acknowledge it, or to think of it. A good or evil affection is shut when we cease to act according to it. The mind, like the material body, is a series of organic spiritual forms. They open or close according to the influences which act upon them. They are under the control of the will, like the eye, and we can open or shut them at our pleasure. When we enter our closets to pray we should shut the door against all worldly and selfish considerations. This means more than at first may appear. It implies that we exclude worldly and selfish motives from our prayers; that we ask primarily only for spiritual and heavenly blessings, and that we desire natural blessings only so far as they can be kept subordinate to our regeneration and the development of a heavenly character.

These directions are not limited to formal and stated prayer, though they apply specifically to it. They apply to the whole of life. We carry this inner chamber with us into all our business, into our recreations and pleasures. Our real prayer is the motives from which we act. From those motives arise constant aspirations. We really " pray without ceasing." The lovers of self and the world are more devout and assiduous in their devotions than Christians. They enter their closets and shut their door against the light of truth, against their neighbor, against the Lord, and open it wide to every breath of influence which favors their selfish and worldly designs. If we desire to gain heaven and win the blessings of eternal life, we must be as careful to shut the door against evil and falsity; we must exclude the desire to be seen of men, and we must open the door wide to the Lord, to our neighbors, and to every heavenly influence. It must be our highest and habitual aspiration to be useful to others in whatever station or employment we may be placed, to be obedient to the Divine truth, and submissive to the Divine will.

5. "And when thou hast shut thy door, pray to thy Father in secret." We have entered the inner chamber of the soul and shut the door. We have shut out our natural thoughts and affections; we have left the labor and the strife, the vain ambitions and foolish vanities of the world; we have ceased to think how men will regard us; we have shut the door behind us, and we are alone. No, not alone. There is a veiled presence filling the chamber with all the light and love we can bear. Who is He? He is not an inconceivable and infinite Being of whom we can form no conception. He is not a stern, majestic, and awful Sovereign, impatient with our ignorance, wearied

with our follies, and burning with fierce indignation against us for our sins. He is not an inexorable judge demanding vengeance upon us as enemies, and exacting the uttermost farthing for our transgressions. Who, then, is He? He is our *Father.* Father!—a name which, even with our earthly imperfections, embodies the tenderest and noblest qualities of human nature. Our father watched over us in infancy and childhood; labored from day to day and year to year to provide us with food and clothing and a comfortable and pleasant home; rejoiced at every indication of awakening intelligence; his heart trembled with fear at every danger which threatened our life; he mourned over our waywardness and youthful follies; he provided us with teachers, and freely gave care, time, and money to prepare us to perform the duties and to gain the rewards of life. There is no other name, unless it be that of mother,—and the Divine Fatherhood combines all the qualities of both father and mother,—which embodies so much kindness, patience, forbearance, and devotion; so much tenderness, wise care, efficient service, unselfish affection, and unchanging love. But the most perfect human father is but a faint shadow, a hint of the infinite perfections of the Father we enter the closet to meet.

6. "Pray to thy Father in secret." If we have followed our Lord's directions we have shut the door against all selfish, worldly, and merely natural considerations; we have excluded all desire to be seen of men; we have entered into the most secret and hidden motives of our life, into the centre and source of our actions. In those and according to those secret desires we must pray. The attitude and the words, and the outer courts of memory and intelligence are regarded only as means of expression.

The prayer is in the secret purpose. It is an internal speech. " Prayer," says Swedenborg, " considered in itself is speaking with God, and at such time there is a certain internal intuition of those things which are the objects of prayer, to which corresponds something like influx into the perception or thought of him who prays, so that there is a kind of opening of man's internals towards God." When we consider that all our life is a constant gift from the Lord, and that it flows into the soul in ceaseless currents from the fountain of life as the warmth of the sun into the secret germs of the seed, we can see something of the nature of genuine prayer, and how it becomes the means of refreshing and vitalizing all our spiritual faculties; we can understand why our Lord spent so much of His time in prayer. When we pray in secret there is an opening of the most interior organic vessels of the will and the affections to the reception of life influent from the Lord. The germ-vessels which when formed become affections, understanding, thought, and act, and all the intellectual and moral faculties which constitute the human mind, open to the Lord and become penetrated, imbued, and quickened with finer qualities and more potent forces of life. It is an enlargement of the vessels which first receive and then conduct the currents of life.

The Lord dwells within us; it is from within that He gets access to us, and builds up His kingdom. Here the work of regeneration begins; we are born from above or within. He stands at every door in this inner chamber of the soul, and knocks for admission. When we open the door by sincere and earnest prayer, He comes in and sups with us and we with Him; that is, He communicates the life of His love to us, and we receive it and reciprocate it. This inner chamber is the large **upper room** where the Lord directs us to make ready that He may eat the passover with us. Here we commune with the Lord. Here we eat the bread which cometh down from heaven and giveth life unto the world; here we drink of that water which becomes in us a well of water springing up into eternal life. The Lord dwells in a region of the soul entirely above our consciousness. There the transfer of the forces of life from the Lord to us takes place; there His love becomes our love, His wisdom our wisdom, His good our good. The work which is done in these secret chambers of the soul, therefore, is of more importance to our spiritual growth and happiness than all outward attainment and possessions. If the doors of this inner chamber are open to the Lord He can flood the soul with the quickening forces of His life. If they are closed He can only reach us in a roundabout external way, and with forces far weaker and containing less of the pure elements of life. Let us heed the Divine directions, and pray to the Father in secret.

7. But "in secret" applies to the Lord as well as to man. "The secret things belong unto the Lord our God." There are infinite treasures of love and wisdom in Him of which we know nothing, and can know nothing except so far as they are revealed to us, and they can only be revealed to us as we come into a state to receive them. We are surrounded with secrets and mysteries on every side. The wisest have penetrated but little beneath the surface of things. How little we know of the secret processes which are going on in ceaseless order and harmony within our material bodies! How much less of the still more complex and wonderful movements in our mental organism, by

which we are able to love and know, to increase in knowledge, and preserve a consciousness of our being!

When we begin our existence we know nothing of the peace and rest, the keen and thrilling ecstasy of the joys which are hidden in the secret qualities of love. We catch glimpses of it in the blessings we enjoy, it brightens our understandings and rejoices our hearts. But there are infinite treasures of it in the secret chambers of the Divine nature, which the Lord desires to bestow upon His children, and which He does bestow upon all in as large and rich measures as they can receive. We enter into the secrets of knowledge by learning, and there are no limits to the worlds of truth which lie before us and whose secrets it will be a joy to explore. We enter into the secrets of the Divine love by receiving that love into our hearts and passing it on in kind and useful deeds to men. The more unselfishly, purely, ardently we love, the more fully and deeply we shall enter into the secrets of the Divine love and taste of its blessedness.

8. "And thy Father which seeth in secret shall reward thee openly." "Who seeth in secret." The quality and efficacy of every prayer is measured by the degree that it is offered in secret. The Lord is present in the secret chambers of the soul, which, as I have said, are the essential ends and motives of all our actions. The Lord looks to the motive, and sees in it all the effects which will result from carrying it into operation. He does not listen to the words uttered, whether they be few or many; whether they flow in eloquent periods, or are stammered forth in broken sentences from the ignorant publican, or the lisping lips of infancy. His ear is in the secret chambers, and He hears only what is uttered there. He

does not hear the affected tone. He does not see the deferential air; the bowed head, the bended knee, the prescribed forms. He is looking in the heart, and He sees only what takes place there. Even the angels who are attendant upon man to guard him from evil and lead him to good do not hear his words, or see his deeds, or know his thoughts. They act only upon his affections, they see only his purposes, and seek to guide him by them. How much more must this be true of the Lord who dwells in the inmost and first principles of thought and deed, and by purifying and elevating the ends of life, and imbuing them with heavenly love, seeks to lead man into heavenly happiness!

" He sees in secret." He sees all the effects and consequences which must follow from every inmost principle of life. All effects are stored up in their causes. The ends, purposes, motives of action, are the closets or treasuries in which all the good we shall ever enjoy, or the sorrows and torments we shall ever suffer, are stored up, and the Lord sees them there. They are there as the tree with its leaves, blossoms, and fruit are in the seed. From one grain of wheat all the harvests in the world could be produced. Some of the lower and microscopic forms of animal life are remarkably rapid in their propagation. But the germs of spiritual fruits, whether they are good or evil, are much more prolific, and they multiply to eternity. They combine with other causes to purify or corrupt them, and their effects become varied and multiplied without end. These results, whether good or evil, are not effected by any arbitrary or mechanical action. They are not bestowed as rewards nor inflicted as punishments. They are orderly and necessary effects from legitimate causes. They grow out of them as the plant out of the seed, according to immutable law. We know that there is something in the secret closets of every seed which determines the kind of fruit it will bear. So there is in every affection or purpose of the will the germs of deeds, the causes of joys or sorrows, which can be multiplied without limit.

We cannot see even natural fruit in the germ. We learn from observation and experience that like produces like in the vegetable and animal kingdoms. But give to the most learned scientist a seed wholly unlike any one he has ever seen or heard of before, and he cannot tell you what fruit it will bear. He may weigh it, analyze it, decompose it, examine it with the most powerful microscope, but he cannot discover the form of the plant which will grow out of it, or the quality of the fruit it will produce. Much less can we see all the results which will flow from cherishing any affection in the inner chambers of the soul. We look at effects; we judge by appearances, and consequently we are subject to constant illusions.

But the Lord "sees in secret." He sees in every innocent and heavenly principle the forms and forces and causes of all the pure and lovely affections, all the sweet and fragrant influences, all the bright joys and blissful rest which will grow out of it. Take, for example, love to Him as a motive of action in all the duties and relations of life. He sees in it the germs of every good it is possible for a finite being to possess and enjoy. He sees in it openness to reception of life from Himself; He sees in it the essential principles of heavenly order; He sees in it conjunction and communion with Himself, a readiness to yield to the Divine attractions of His own love, by which we are drawn into more intimate and vital relations with Him and closer to His infinite heart; He sees in it beauty of person such as mortal eyes have never beheld, power of which we have never dreamed, intelligence of which the highest angel has no knowledge, joys beyond all human power to conceive, an order, a harmony, a rest, a peace, a blessedness which surpasses all human vision or capacity of hope. He sees infinite blessings of which we have no idea and no name; delights which cannot be expressed in human language. They are secrets to us which we can only penetrate as we receive that love, and according to the measure of our ability embody it in deeds. But they are all clear in the light of His infinite intelligence. Oh, that we were not so blind, and stupid, and inexpressibly foolish as to close our hearts against that love which contains in its very substance and nature the promise and potency of all the good which it is possible for infinite love and wisdom to give, or man with his limitless possibilities to receive!

9. And thy Father which seeth in secret shall reward thee openly." There is a profounder meaning and a richer promise embodied in the words, "shall reward thee openly" than appears upon the surface. The word our Lord used and which is translated "reward" means much more than compensation for a service arbitrarily bestowed. It means to make a complete and adequate return; to grant all that is claimed or looked for; and when spoken in relation to the Lord it means to give all that is asked and hoped for; all that it is possible for the suppliant to receive in the present and in the future. When we go into our closets, shut the door to self and the world and open them to the Lord, we bring ourselves into vital conjunction with Him,

and the currents of His life begin to flow into the organic forms of our natures. We may be able to receive but a small measure of that life at first. But it is essentially creative in its nature; it enlarges the vessels which receive it, and makes them more capacious to receive larger measures of life. It tends to perfect the quality of the inmost forms of our being and give them the power of receiving finer forms of life. Consequently the reward is constantly increasing, and it will continue to do so forever. Suppose you ask in humble and heartfelt sincerity that the Lord's kingdom may come in you, and that His will may be done on the earth of your natural mind as it is in the heaven of the spiritual mind; you place yourself in such relations to the Lord that He can begin to answer the prayer. He answers it according to the measure of your ability to receive the answer. It may take Him all your life to answer it fully, even according to your own expectations. It will take Him to eternity to answer it according to His. But He begins the answer; He makes a full return of all you ask; but in making it He gives you power to ask and to receive more. And this process will continue to eternity. We always receive as much as we ask. I do not mean as much as we ask in words. Millions of prayers are offered every day with the lips for the sanctification of the heart and the regeneration of humanity. But very few are offered in the closet, and those that are offered there are answered in the degree that man can receive the answer.

10. But the Lord not only promises to reward the sincere prayer, but to do it openly. You will observe that there is a parallelism and contrast between hypocritical and genuine prayer. The prayer of the hypocrite is made

in the most conspicuous places, to be seen of men, and the
reward is expected from them.  The genuine prayer is
made in the closet, to the Heavenly Father, and the promise is an open reward.  The vain prayer is made with
many words, with the hope of being heard for much speaking.  The sincere prayer is made in secret; may not be
voiced; may be a mute appeal, a despairing cry, an internal
effort to turn to the Lord, an aspiration of the heart for
a higher life, a more intimate communion with Him.
Both have their reward.  One comes from without, and
gives a momentary delight which turns in the end to a
curse.  The other comes from within, from perennial
sources, and increases in richness and fulness forever.
But you may desire to know in what way the Lord rewards us openly.  He does it according to an immutable
law of His divine order, a law which we see in our own
lives in everything we do.  All the forces of life, all the
causes of our joys and sorrows, come from within.  Every
deed is first an affection, then a thought, then a natural
act.  The springs of conduct rise in the secret closets of
the soul as the streams which refresh and beautify the
earth gush forth from the secret chambers of the hills.
When we open the affections to the Lord in sincere prayer,
He imbues them with new and finer qualities; He enlarges and purifies them, and they flow down through all
the degrees of the mind, enriching and enlarging them.
They give delicacy, acuteness, and perception to the
understanding.  Thought is affection formed, affection
brought out into distinct consciousness.  Every thought
which passes through our minds is the form of some affection to which it gives body and existence.  The affection
dwells in the thought or in truth, and uses it to come

out more openly into speech and deed. When our affections become enlarged and purified, we gain a new degree of vital power; and the new purpose gives a new direction and a new quality to our deeds. A heavenly affection gives tone to the voice, beauty to the face, loveliness to our actions, and a new charm to every faculty of mind and body. You cannot go into your closet and shut the door and offer a sincere prayer to the Lord for any heavenly good, and conceal from your friends the reward you will receive. Your face will begin to shine as the face of Moses did when he came down from the mount. You have been in the mount with the Lord. You will be more earnest and unselfish in purpose; you will have wider and more tender sympathies with every form of human suffering; you will be more devoted to your friends; more faithful in your employments; wiser and more generous in your charities; and your influence on all around you will be purer and more elevating.

We can see many beautiful effects in this life of the transfiguring power of these spiritual and Divine influences. But while we are clothed in the garments of clay we can see but little more than the shadow of them. Their harmonies come faintly to our dulled ears, and their lovely forms are seen but dimly through the clouds of sense. But when we are released from this imprisonment in the material body and rise into the clear light of the spiritual world, then every heavenly affection which we had made our own by life, and which is stored up in the secret chambers of the soul, will come out into open manifestation. These secret communings with our Heavenly Father will determine the heaven we enter, the society which will welcome us to its association, the friends who will greet us, and the home we shall dwell in forever.   A new influx of the Divine love, which enters our souls when we open their secret chambers in prayer, will continue to work in us and come out openly without and around us forever.   It will add force to the attraction which draws us to the pure and good, and which conjoins us with the Lord; it will be a new light in our sky, a new beauty in our home, a new charm in every object which adorns it, and it will endow us with a finer and more delicate sense, with a keener perception and a larger capacity for enjoyment.   It will be a deeper peace, a brighter joy, a sweeter communion, a more blissful rest.

# V

## THE PROPER OBJECT OF WORSHIP.

---

*"After this manner therefore pray ye: Our Father which art in the Heavens."*—Matthew vi. 9.

IN the preceding verses which we have already considered, our Lord has taught us what motives and methods to avoid in prayer, when and how to offer our petitions, and He has given us the assurance, if we follow these directions, of a full and open reward. He offers every encouragement to come freely to the "Father who seeth in secret," and open our inmost desires to Him. He seeks to win our confidence, and with paternal kindness He asks us to make known to Him our wants, our sorrows, and our joys. He sympathizes with us in all our difficulties, labors, and temptations; helps us in every struggle with evil, and rejoices with us in every victory over our selfish and worldly desires. If we could realize, even in a remote degree, how forbearing, how patient, how gentle, how kind He is, how deeply He desires to help and bless us, we should not be so reluctant and formal in going to Him for sympathy and guidance, and pouring into His

75

compassionate ear the sorrows and the joys of our hearts. We all need help; we all long for sympathy. There is no greater comfort in this cold and selfish world, no treasure more precious than a friend who fully appreciates us, and to whom we can unbosom ourselves with the perfect assurance of being understood, and from whom we can get the wisest counsel and the deepest consolation. The Lord is such a friend, though infinitely wiser, tenderer, truer, and more considerate than any earthly friend,—than the wisest father or the most loving mother. These qualities will appear more clearly as we enter into the deep and genuine import of the prayer He has taught us.

"After this manner therefore pray ye." We are not to understand by this direction that we are to limit our petitions to these words. The Lord gives us the manner, the spirit, the scope of our prayers. We must pray in this simple, direct, and unostentatious way. We may make our prayers as specific as we please. Sometimes one want will press upon us and absorb our whole thought. We are in distress, in the agony of some conflict; we are overwhelmed by some great sorrow and we can only say, " If it be possible, let this cup pass from me." We are in despair; we seem to be deserted by men and forsaken by the Lord, and we can only cry, " My God, my God, why hast Thou forsaken me!" Then, again, we have met with some great deliverance by which the soul is filled with peace and rest, and our lips can but feebly express the gratitude and praise which thrills our hearts. But every want which we can feel, every desire of which the heart is capable, every good it is possible for the human mind to conceive, or the lips to ask, is comprehended in the few brief petitions of this prayer, and the more fully we enter into its infinite depths, the more clearly we shall see that it comprises all our needs, from the lowest to the highest.

First, the Lord teaches us to whom we must offer our prayers, and how we are to conceive of Him. "Our Father." We are to think of Him as our father. There is nothing more simple, tender, and kind than this. Every child can understand it. The Lord does not ask us to conceive of the inconceivable, to think of Him as He is in Himself; that no finite being can do. He does not ask us to know the unknowable, to comprehend an infinite essence. He comes to us in what we know. He comes to us in the simplest and most familiar form. The relation of father is one of the first conceptions by which the little child distinguishes one man from another. There is a class of learned men at the present day who call themselves agnostics, or spiritual know-nothings. They do not deny that there may be a God, and a spiritual world, and a life after the death of the body, but they have no belief upon these subjects, because they do not know anything about them, and they conceive all knowledge of them in our present state to be impossible. They cannot conceive of an infinite Being, and, therefore, they do not believe in one. The principle which lies at the root of their denial seems to be, disbelief in what we cannot fully comprehend; but, if this principle was made of universal application, we should not believe in anything, for we cannot fully comprehend the simplest things. The most profound scientist cannot comprehend how we see or hear; how a blade of grass grows. He may know much of the means by which these effects are produced; but why they produce them he cannot tell. We only look upon the surface of things. The most learned man is as igno-

rant of inmost causes as the little child.   We cannot fully
comprehend one another; but we can know something,
and know that with certainty.   A little child knows but
little about its father; but it knows enough to initiate
and define its relations to him.   As its understanding
and affections become enlarged, it will know more.   The
little serves the present purpose and leads to more.

The Lord takes the simple, universal relation of fatherhood, and by means of it leads us to Himself; instructs us
to think of Him as a father.   We can form no idea of
God except by means of what we know of men.   If there
is no likeness, no inherent and essential relation between
the Lord and man, we can gain no idea of Him.   What
do we know of love, or mercy, or wisdom, or of any of the
attributes we ascribe to the Lord, but from what we have
learned of their nature as they exist in ourselves, or as we
have seen them manifested in others?   Nothing.   To
ascribe these qualities to Him, therefore, unless they are
of the same nature as they are in us, conveys no idea of
Him.   They do not apply to Him; they are an empty
sound signifying nothing; they are worse: they are mis-
leading; they deceive us.   In our thought we attribute to
the Lord qualities which do not belong to Him.   All that
we can say or think of Him is simply a delusion.

But if man was made in the image and after the likeness of God, if the Divine nature was finited in man, then
human qualities give us a hint of Divine qualities; human
relations give us a true idea of our relations to the Lord,
and by means of them the Lord can instruct us in Divine
knowledge, and lead us to know Him "whom to know
aright is life everlasting."   In this Divine prayer He instructs us to think of Him as a father, to pray to Him as

a father, to trust Him as a father, and we must give to the word, father, its genuine meaning. If we begin by divesting it of all the forms, qualities, and relations which belong to a human father, we vacate it of all meaning. Let us take this human relationship, then, and follow its essential qualities to their legitimate conclusions. If we do we must find the Being to whom we are to direct our prayers.

A father is a personal being in the human form. He is one being in one person. The Father in the heavens must be one Being in one Divine Person, and that Person must be in the human form. It is impossible to conceive of a father in any other form, or as a mere abstract essence. The father of a human being must be a man, and a man without the human form is impossible. The Father whom we are to love, and whom we are to meet in prayer in the inner chamber of the soul, must be in the human form, and He has revealed Himself to us in that form in Jesus Christ.

By the Father is generally understood Jehovah, the Divine Being as He is in Himself. Consequently Christians generally address their prayers to Him. But the human mind is incapable of forming any idea of Jehovah, as He is in Himself. We cannot approach Him in thought or affection. There is no access to Him possible except through His Divine Humanity. Jehovah as He is in Himself is above the heavens, above all created and finite forms, beyond all human conception. We must keep in mind that prayer is not merely a matter of words. One may repeat all the words ever addressed to the Lord, and not offer a prayer. Prayer is a real communion of the human soul with the Lord; it is the opening of the affections to the reception of the forces of life from Him. There

must, therefore, be conjunction of mind with mind.    To
effect this there must be adaptation and adjustment.    But
there can be no direct contact between the Divine as it is
in itself and any finite form.    Even the sun, as it is in
itself, cannot come in direct contact with the plant in a
way to produce vegetable growth.    It must be modified
and adapted; its rays must be tempered by atmospheres
and by the earth, before they take effect upon the seed and
cause it to grow.    How much more impossible it must be
for man to approach and to receive into himself the awful
forces of the Divine life!

We cannot approach or conceive of a human being as
he is in himself.    We can only form some idea of men and
women as to their inmost and essential character as it is
revealed to us through the medium of the material body.
How much less can we form any conception of the uncreated Divine life as it is in itself?    We cannot gain any
conception of the nature of a fruit even as it exists in the
seed.    The inmost forms must clothe themselves with the
flesh and blood, the pulp and juices of the fruit, before
we can tell whether they are sweet or sour, good or harmful.    If we cannot judge of the essential qualities of the
lowest things until they clothe themselves with a proper
medium by which they can act upon our senses, and in
that way reveal themselves to us, how much less can the
infinite First Cause of the creation and of all created beings, reveal Himself to our consciousness without appropriate mediums?

No.    When we look at the subject as it is, we can see
that we cannot pray to Jehovah, the Father above the
heavens.    We can use words; we can say Jehovah, God,
but the words are not the prayer.    The prayer is the

process which goes on in the closet; the internal turning and opening of the affections, and the perception, the thought, the idea which results from the entrance of the Lord into the closet.

We can form some idea of Jehovah as He has revealed Himself to us in the human nature which He assumed and made Divine. Jesus Christ is the Father in a human form, adapted to human conception. The Father and Son are one person, as the soul and body are one man. The Father and Son are not the same plane or degree of the Divine personality, as the soul and body are not the same plane or degree of our personality. It requires many degrees and forms to make a man. Look at the material body for example. It is composed of many bodies in the human form. The bones, the arteries and veins, the nerves, are all in the human form. Each one constitutes a body by itself. But it requires them all to make the human body. And besides these material forms, it requires the soul and the spiritual body to make a man. All these different spiritual degrees and organic forms are parts of the one being.

So the Father and the Son are not two persons, two beings; nor is one a Divine being and the other simply a human being. Both make one Divine Being. This our Lord Himself declares in the most positive manner. " I and my Father are one." One what? One man? or one God? If they are one man, then there is no God. If they are one God, then we have a God who is the centre and source of life, in His inmost nature entirely above all human conception, but who has also a human nature in which He reveals Himself to human consciousness, in which He comes down to human apprehension. " He

6

that hath seen me, hath seen the Father. How then say-
est thou, Show us the Father." This is the same as to
say, Where will you look for Him except in me? In what
form do you expect to find Him except in the one in
which He has appeared to you? " Believe in me," He
says; "I am in the Father, and the Father in me." The
Divine and the human interpenetrate each other in my
person, as the soul and body interpenetrate each other in
every man. The soul, as we all acknowledge, is in the
body. So our Lord's soul, which is called by the name
Father, dwelt in His body. A man's body is in his soul,
also, though not in precisely the same sense as the soul is
in the body. The body is not in the soul, as water is in a
vessel, as blood is in the arteries. It is in the sphere of
its active forces. It is in it as a plant is in the heat of the
sun, and the heat of the sun is in it. It is penetrated, infilled, suffused with it. So the Human nature was penetrated, infilled, suffused, glorified, and became one with the
Divine nature: and both together, each within the other,
make one Divine Being. " Our Father in the Heavens"
is this glorified Humanity, in which the infinite First
Cause, the incomprehensible and primal Source of all
being, comes out from His infinity and manifests Himself
to His children in a personal, glorious, Divine, human form.

We are not, then, to think of the Father to whom we
pray as a diffused essence, as an omnipresent force, but as a
glorious Divine Man in the human form; as the same
Being who was incarnated, who healed human diseases,
who instructed the ignorant, who as to His human nature
suffered, and was crucified. When He dwelt in a material
body He was our Father on the earth. Now He is risen
and glorified, He is our Father in the heavens.

The necessity for having a distinct object, a distinct personal form in our minds when we pray, is vastly more important than we generally suppose. It is for the want of this that prayer is so unmeaning and ineffectual. As Swedenborg has said, there can be no conjunction with an invisible, abstract essence. The thought has nothing to rest upon. It passes off into empty space, like the light which does not reach any recipient object. Think of a child asking help, or a blessing, from the abstract qualities of a father! In what a different state of mind we ask a favor of a man from that in which we ask blessings of the Lord! If we have a distinct personal being in our minds of whom we know something, to whom we are related, who possesses what we want, whose character we know, whom we know where to find, and how to address, the way is clear before us, and our praying will have some purpose.

All these requisites to genuine prayer we have, when we go to the Lord Jesus Christ, and think of Him alone, without any mental reservations, or any effort to go behind Him, and to think of some being distinct from Him. We can fix our thoughts upon Him, as He appeared to Peter, James, and John when he was transfigured before them, when " His face did shine as the sun, and His raiment was white as the light."

Having gained a clear and distinct idea of the personal Being whom we are to address in prayer, the next of inquiry which demands our attention is, what paternal qualities we shall attribute to Him. Father is not a general term implying no more than that the Lord is the creator of the human race. Every word of Scripture has a universal meaning; that is, it applies to every particular to which it relates ; to the least things as well as to the greatest. It is not limited by time or place or special relation. We are to take the term Father in its universal sense; we are to infil it with all the qualities, and with the highest qualities of fatherhood we can conceive, and when we have done that, we shall fall infinitely short of the reality. But let us particularize :

1. Our natural fathers are only instruments in the Lord's hands to perpetuate and enlarge the creation of human beings. In this respect, as in all acts of natural creation, we are merely instrumental means. In the production of our harvests, the husbandman is only one link in the vast chain of causes and effects by which the end is reached. The Lord is the Creator and Father of every form of vegetable and of animal life. If, therefore, we take the lowest idea of fatherhood, the Lord is our primary and real father, our father upon the earth.

2. But before we can enter the kingdom of heaven we must be born again, born from above ; the spiritual degrees of the mind must be formed ; the new heavens and the new earth must be created ; and this is effected without any special, direct intervention of others. In the formation of this heavenly mind, the Lord is more especially our Father ; we are born of God. In this degree of our being we are created into His image and likeness ; we bear the impress of His form and character which show our lineage ; we become His children and heirs of His infinite riches. Oh that we could gain such a clear conception of this glorious truth that it would seem to us to be as it is, a most positive reality! How proud men are of noble descent! How delighted they are to know that they have blue blood in their veins ! We do not see so much of this ancestral

worship as is found in those countries where a titled nobility exists. But the principle is native to the human heart. And there are just grounds for it. It is fortunate to be well born. Blood tells. The virtues as well as the iniquities of the fathers descend to the children.

Now apply this law of the Divine Order to the case before us. The Lord teaches us to call Him "our Father," and what He directs us to call Him He seeks to become. Here open to us the grand possibilities of our being. Let us not pass the subject by as an unmeaning one, or the possession as unattainable. The Lord is our Father! We can claim our descent from Him. We can become the finite forms of His love. That love which is the infinite source of all life can become our life, the germinal principle of our characters; our hearts can beat responsive to it, our affections can be animated with its warmth; imbued with its purity, our understanding can be moulded into the form of the Divine wisdom, become the embodiment of His beauty, and illuminated with His truth. Our whole spiritual forms can be so impressed with the infinite perfections of the Divine Character that our parentage will be evident to every beholder. It can be seen in the clear and lovely lines of the face. It can be proclaimed in pure tones in the voice. It can be discerned in every motion of the body swayed to grace and dignity by the indwelling spirit hereditarily derived from our Father in the Heavens.

There can be no nobler birth than this. What is the ancestry of kings and emperors compared with this? If it is a cause for gratitude and joy to be able to look back through a long line of progenitors, and find in it great and wise men, pure and lovely women, how much greater cause

have we to rejoice that we can claim the Lord for our
Father, and become heirs to the everlasting and ever-increasing glory and blessedness which He delights to bestow
upon His children; and which He does bestow upon them,
just in the degree that they become His children and are
able to receive His blessings!

Having thus gained a distinct idea that the Lord is
our Father, essentially the Father of our bodies and natural minds, and specifically the Father of our souls, if we
have "been born from above," let us try to fill that term
with all the perfections of the paternal relation possible to
our conception. We shall find them all in Him, and infinitely more.

1. A good father will provide according to the best of
his ability for the support and physical comfort of his
children. Has not our Heavenly Father done this? He
has filled the world with substances for the support of the
body; for its sustenance, clothing, and comfort. The
harvests of the world are His gifts. In what lovely forms
He presents these provisions of His love! He is not content to give us the substance alone in a shapeless mass:
He gathers His gifts into purple clusters; He moulds
them into beautiful fruits; He dyes them with lovely
colors; He fills them with delicate aromas; He makes
them savory, and sweet. ·In supplying one want He gratifies
every sense; He makes every step of their creation beautiful.
The stem which bears them is beautiful in form, and then
He clothes it with a garniture of green, glorifies it with
the beauty of blossoms, and crowns it with a diadem of
fruit. Is He not a provident and bountiful Father?

2. A good father will provide for the instruction of his
children. Our Heavenly Father has so arranged His

provisions for our natural support that they shall be the constant means of intellectual and moral cultivation. All our industrial, domestic, social, and civil relations are means of developing our affections and enlarging our understandings. Our best lessons are learned in the school of the family, in the school of labor, and in the school of society. But, besides these schools and teachers, He has given us His prophets, and He has come Himself to teach us the lessons we could not learn from nature and from each other. He has left nothing untried or undone which it was possible for infinite love and wisdom to do to teach us our true nature and destiny and the best means of attaining it. Does He not, therefore, possess this paternal excellence in the highest degree?

3. A good father is patient and gentle, kind and wise. He will withhold as well as give; he will restrain and guide. The Lord is infinitely kind and gentle and patient. "His mercy is forever." "As a father pitieth his children, so the Lord pitieth them that fear Him." He waits for us with an infinite patience; He loves us with an infinite love; He watches over us with an omniscient eye, and omits no occasion to confer upon every one of His children the greatest blessings He can persuade them to receive. Take any parental quality you choose and exalt it to the greatest excellence you can conceive, and our Father in the Heavens is all that and infinitely more. There is no quality which could entitle Him to the name of Father which He does not possess.

But there is one respect in which He is entitled to the claim in an eminent degree. Our earthly parents become less our parents as we advance in life. Children become less dependent upon them. Parents can do less for them.

The ties which bind them together grow weaker, and parent and child grow away from each other. But our Father in the Heavens will become more and more our Father to eternity. We shall be growing into His likeness; we shall become more fully His children. He will continually create us anew. The marks of our lineage will become more distinct. We shall become larger embodiments of His love, and continually advance into the beauty of His image and the glory of His wisdom. There is no other hope so grand; no other possibility of attainment so blessed as this.

"*Our* Father." The Lord does not teach us to say my Father, but our Father. There is a grand significance in this. It sweeps away human distinctions and reverses human judgments. When we offer this prayer, we place ourselves on the level of a common parentage, we confess a common humanity. The king in his palace, clothed in rich attire and surrounded with elegance and beauty and abundant means to minister to every desire, kneels at a cushioned altar and says, " Our Father." The peasant in his hut, clad in coarse and soiled garments, sheltered from storms only by rough and naked walls, in the midst of rude and scanty furniture, clasps hands hardened by toil and utters the same words, " Our Father." The most learned scientist, the most skilful artist, the genius, the hero, whose praise is upon all lips, and the little child whose eyes are just opening to the wonders of the universe, or the most unlettered laborer, must address the same Being in the same words: they must say, " Our Father." The rich and the poor, however widely separated by external conditions, must ignore them all when they enter the closet or kneel in the house of worship. They must utter the words which confess a common parentage, a common nature, and fraternal relations. The artificial and merely natural distinctions which men and women estimate so highly, and on the possession of which they assume so much superiority, do not appear before the Lord. He looks only upon the heart, and estimates us by what He sees there. We are His children; we are brethren, and nobly born, in the degree that we are created in His likeness and partake of His nature. In the light of this truth, how all merely natural distinctions fade away! Can you pray this prayer? You can say the words with your lips. Can you enter the closet, and shut the door against all natural and artificial distinctions and say, with the understanding and from the heart, " Our Father"? Only in the degree you come into this state do you pray " after this manner."

" Our Father who art in the Heavens." Why, heavens? Because there is more than one heaven, and we can only pray to the Father in the heaven in which we are. Every human being has in possibility three planes, or degrees of his spiritual nature, entirely distinct from one another. These degrees of the mind constitute the heavens within him. The one which becomes opened and formed is the one in which the Lord dwells; it is the one in which we think, in which we love and live. The heaven we shall consciously enter when we throw aside the veil of flesh will correspond with the one which has become formed within us. It is in the heavens within us that the Lord becomes our Father. As these heavens are formed by learning the truth and living according to it, He comes in and dwells with us and we with Him. Our real worship consists in the opening and creation of one of these degrees of the spiritual mind. There He builds the mansions in which we are to dwell with Him forever. If only the lowest degree is opened, we shall enter the corresponding heaven. We shall find our home there, and the Lord will be our Father there, according to the measure of our knowledge and love. If the second degree of the mind is opened, we shall rise into the light and glory of the second heaven and live and love and worship our Father as He can manifest Himself to us in that degree. If the inmost degree is opened, we shall live in that, and enter into the fullest and most blissful joys it is possible for a finite being to experience.

It is not, therefore, without a meaning specifically applicable to us that our Lord teaches us to address Him as Our Father in the *Heavens.* It is an acknowledgment of His Fatherhood by every one in the degree he is becoming regenerated. Every angel can use it with special application to himself. It is also a prayer that we may become His children; that we may become more innocent, more childlike, more pliant to the brooding power of His love; that we may become gentler in spirit, stronger in affection, nobler in action, purer in life, and in all respects more like our Father in the Heavens, into whose image and likeness He is in the constant effort to create us.

# VI.

## HALLOWING THE LORD'S NAME.

_____

*"Hallowed be Thy Name."*—Matthew vi. 9.

THE Lord's instructions concerning prayer are based upon a perfect knowledge of man's nature and relations to the Source of his life. They are complete in every respect; they are adequate to every human condition and to every human want. This perfection of instruction is not limited to guiding us to the Person whom we must address, nor to the petitions we offer: they extend to the order and relative importance of our requests. The first in importance is the first in desire and thought. Prayer necessarily implies a Personal Being to whom we offer our supplications. It implies some knowledge of that Being, and some belief that He can hear and answer our prayers. We are, therefore, first directed to the true object of worship; we are taught where to find Him, and how to conceive of Him. We are taught to regard Him as "our Father;" and not only as our Father as a First Cause, as an incomprehensible essence, or an omnipotent force, but as our Father in the heavens, as the Author and Giver of every good and truth, of every blessing which it is possible for man to receive. We are taught to come to Him with the freedom and trust of children in a revered and wise and loving father, freely make known our wants, and ask for the help, consolation, and guidance we need.

Then He teaches us the primary and essential end of all prayer. He reveals the spirit in which we should come to our Father, the motives which should lead us to pray, the first and essential good which we should desire and seek above all others. That law of the Divine order, that root-principle and essential cause of all true knowledge of the Divine nature, of our own nature, and of the means of complete and enduring happiness, is revealed in the words, "Hallowed be Thy Name." That is the first heavenly grace to seek, the first good to ask, because every other good is contained in it, and grows out of it as an effect from its cause. The Lord's kingdom cannot come, either in our own souls or in human society, until we hallow His name. His will cannot be done on the earth as it is in heaven until His name is hallowed on the earth as it is in heaven. He can only give us our daily bread as we hallow His name. The life we shall live, and the good we shall receive in this world and through eternity, will be determined in quality and degree by the measure in which we hallow the Lord's name. It becomes, therefore, of the utmost moment to know what is meant by His name, and how we can hallow it. To this subject your devout attention is invited. It is a matter of so much importance, and we are so prone to rest in mere appearances, and find it so difficult to rise above them, that it will richly repay the most careful examination and the best means of illustration we can command.

I. Let us consider the essential meaning of the word " name." It is familiar enough, and we may think we fully comprehend it. But it has a profound significance when applied to the Lord. It means much more than a simple word employed to designate Him, as we give names to persons and things. Names are arbitrary or real. An arbitrary name is an epithet applied to persons or things without any reference to its meaning, as the names we give our children. A real name describes the person or thing to which it is applied. A perfect name would express all the qualities of the object to which it was given. It is derived from the object rather than given to it ; that is, the object suggests the name. All names had their origin in some condition or circumstance or quality of the person or thing named. This is the case with many if not all the names of persons mentioned in the Word. Names were sometimes given to persons by Divine direction, as in the case of John the Baptist and of our Lord. The names of many of the principal men were given to them from some circumstance connected with their birth, or the work they performed, or the character they represented. Names were changed to denote some change in the special relations of those who bore them. We apply to men names to represent their office and character, and we change them to denote any change in these respects.

All the names applied to the Supreme Being are real ones ; that is, they express some quality or attribute of the Divine character, or some relation to the universe or to men. He is called Jehovah, which means the same as I AM, and expresses inmost, essential, self-existing Being. And as He is love itself, Jehovah denotes the Divine Love. God denotes the Divine existence, which is love in form ;

and as love gains existence, stands forth to view by means
of truth, God is the name of the Divine truth or wisdom.
These names are often used together; then they denote
the Divine Love and Wisdom. The Lord is called Father
with reference to the human nature, by the assumption
of which He came into the world. Clothed with that nature He becomes Redeemer, Saviour, Immanuel, or God
with us. Regarded from His human nature He is called
Son of God and Son of Man. Jesus Christ is the name
of Jehovah God clothed with a human nature, by means
of which He came down to men, modified the Divine forces
of His love and wisdom, and adapted them to the weakness and waywardness of human affections corrupted by
sin, and the blindness of the human understanding perverted by error. That human nature filled with hereditary tendencies to evil and distorted by many generations
of falsity, He glorified or made Divine, and a perfect
medium of communicating the life of His love and the
truth of His wisdom to men. That Divine Humanity
Jehovah made one with Himself. It is, therefore, the
Divine body in which He dwells; it is the Divine name
by which He is to be known among men. In that form
He is the "Alpha and Omega, the First and the Last."
When His human nature was glorified the prophecy was
fulfilled. "In that day there shall be one Jehovah and
His name one," and that name is Lord. "Ye call me
Lord and Master, and ye do well, for so I am."

A perfect name is one which expresses all the qualities,
attributes, and relations of the person to whom it is given.
It is impossible for any word of material origin to do this.
A material name only calls our attention to the person
designated, or to some special quality which belongs to him.

This is all the help it can give us. A word, or the sound which it represents, is not the real name. The real name by which every person is truly known is his deeds, the forms in which his character manifests itself. " By their fruits ye shall know them." " Actions speak louder than words." A man's deeds express his real character more fully and truly than words. The words we use only serve to call our attention to the deed.

By name, then, we are to understand all that the name suggests and carries with it, not merely the person which it calls up to the consciousness, but all the qualities of the person. This large idea of the meaning of name throws much light upon the significance and use of the term in the Sacred Scriptures. The Lord's name is constantly put for the Lord Himself, and for the attributes of His character. The Lord's name is called excellent, blessed, glorious, reverend, righteous, holy, terrible. Men are called upon to exalt, to praise, to fear, to sanctify, to bless the Lord's name. The most remarkable power is attributed to His name. Enemies are overcome by it, devils are cast out, diseases are cured, deliverances are wrought, and salvation is effected. The Lord gives a name to His people, knows them by name, calls them by name, gives them a new name, writes their names in the book of life; engraves them upon the palms of His hands, and writes His name upon their foreheads. We are taught to ask in His name, and for the sake of His name, and the promise is, that we shall receive everything we ask in His name. The Lord commanded the disciples to baptize in the name of the Father, the Son, and the Holy Spirit. By these examples of the use and meaning of name in the Sacred Scriptures, we are led to the conclusion that by name we are to understand all the attributes and qualities of the Divine Being to whom it is applied.

II. We are now prepared to consider the second part of our subject, Hallowed be Thy Name. What are we to understand by hallowed, and how can we hallow the Lord's name? To hallow is to set apart from common use and consecrate to the Divine service. The original word is translated hallow, or holy. Hallow expresses the action and holy the quality of it. The special questions for consideration, then, are, What quality or state of any being or thing is holiness? How shall we conceive of it? How can we hallow or make holy the Lord's name? The Lord has taught us to pray, " Hallowed be Thy Name." We can not do this without a definite and distinct meaning of the words we employ. You have used the words this morning. What idea did you attach to them? What desire did you express? What request did you make to the Lord? If you had no desire in your heart, and no distinct thought in your mind, you offered no prayer. It was a merely mechanical performance. Let us try to gain a distinct and true idea of the meaning of the words we employ, and use them with that meaning when we pray.

We may regard the subject from a negative, or a positive point of view. Negatively, holiness is freedom from any stain, any taint or imperfection. It is a state in which there is no evil, or falsity. Positively, it is a state of order, harmony, perfection of form, relation and adaptation to all uses, and adequate power to perform them. Purity of character in a human being is freedom from all admixture of evil and falsity. The mind is an organic form as well as the body. Purity of mind, then, is a mental state in proper form and order; a mind in which all the parts act in perfect harmony with each other, and the whole in perfect harmony with the inflowing life of the Lord. There is no discrepancy, no discord. It is a perfect instrument, and if the result of the activities of this instrument were tones they would be pure tones. The results are affections, thoughts, and actions, and if the mind is pure in form, the affections, thoughts, and actions will be pure.

We may consider the question in another way. We use the term pure blood with reference to descent. A pure African is a man or woman who has no white blood in the veins. We apply the same terms with the same meaning to animals. Now man was made in the likeness and image of God; he was made in the same form. He gets the human form from the Lord, and not the Lord the human form from him. The Divine attributes are finited in man. Man as to his spiritual nature was organized by the Divine life, that all the flow of his activities might move in perfect harmony with the Divine activities as one instrument vibrates in harmony with another, so that man's life should be in accord with the Divine life; so that man's love should be a finite form of the Divine love in all its qualities; so that man's understanding should be a finite form and perfect recipient of the Divine truth, and all his thoughts and feelings and actions should accord with the Lord's. He had pure blood in his veins. So long as he maintained his integrity his descent was uncontaminated. He was pure; he was holy in a finite degree, and his purity of form, internal as well as external, and all the attributes of affection, thought, and action, answered to the holiness of the Lord as the finite answers to the infinite. We conclude, therefore, that Holiness in the Lord is wholeness, integrity, infinite perfection of every form.

7

quality, degree, state, and activity, and this holiness becomes wholeness, soundness, integrity, purity, holiness in
man when life is received in the same relative form as
that in which it comes from its Divine source.

Having thus endeavored to get a true idea of holiness,
let us proceed to consider what is meant by hallowing the
Lord's name, or making it holy. By name we understand
all the Lord's attributes in a Divine human form. How
can we make that name holy in Him? What can we do
to make it holy? It is holy now. We cannot add to it,
or take from it in the slightest degree. What, then, does
the petition mean? What does our Lord teach us to ask
when we repeat the words?

1. He teaches us to acknowledge the holiness and
Divinity of His Humanity. This is the essential principle of true Christianity. We can get no true idea of
Jehovah God except as He is embodied and revealed to
us in His Human nature made Divine. On the other
hand, we cannot get a true conception of Jesus Christ if
we regard Him as a merely human being. The Divine
must be regarded from the human, and the human from
the Divine, both of which make the complete and only
Divine Being, as we must judge of man's spiritual nature
from its manifestations in and by means of the material
body, and of the origin, nature, and use of the activities
and functions of the material body, from the soul. The
spirit must be viewed in the body, and the body in the
light of the soul, before we can get a full and complete
idea of a man. We hallow the Lord's name when we set
it apart, or regard it as distinct and above a merely human
finite nature, when we attribute to it all the infinite perfections of Divinity in a human and conceivable form.

The name of Our Father in the heavens is Jesus Christ, or the Divine Humanity. That this is His new name is evident, as He Himself calls it in the Revelation, and as He expressly declares in John, when He says, " Father, glorify Thy name. Then came a voice from heaven, saying, I have both glorified it and will glorify it again." At another time He says, " I have manifested Thy name unto the men which Thou gavest me out of the world." " I have declared unto them Thy name, and will declare it." Here we have a distinct declaration that the Son of God is the name of Jehovah in the humanity, and that it is in and by means of this human nature that the Divine is revealed to men. To declare the name of Jehovah does not mean simply to speak the word, or to tell men that that is the name of the Supreme Being, but to reveal His character and attributes and relations to men. And that is the special purpose for which Jehovah clothed His Divine with a human nature. By " Thy name," then, we are to understand the Divine love, wisdom, power, and all the Divine attributes, as they are manifested in His humanity. We are to conceive of them and think of them as they are revealed to us in Jesus Christ, in all their tenderness, and gentleness, and patience, and perfect adaptation to all man's spiritual needs.

It is of the utmost importance to our spiritual progress and life that we should get this idea of the Lord in as clear and forcible a form as possible. If our conception of the Divine character was clearly and wholly such as it is manifested in Jesus Christ, without any exception, without thinking that there is any other Divine being, or any other Divine qualities, or any other way of regarding men than such as we see revealed in the Lord Jesus Christ, we should come to Him with more assurance. We should feel that every quality and faculty of the Divine nature was wholly on our side. Not merely His mercy, while His justice stood aloof, making demands which we can never satisfy. But that the whole of the Divine nature is favorable to our highest good, and is always ready to save us from sin and to confer upon us every blessing we will receive. If we could feel that when we go to Him we go to an infinite friend whose love can never change, whose wisdom and power have no limit, whose patience we can never exhaust, and who is infinitely more considerate for us than we are for ourselves,—if we could get such a conception of our Father in the heavens, how delightful it would be to go to Him, to pray to Him, to commune with Him, to call Him our Father, and to pour forth all our secrets and our sorrows and our joys into His ear, and to surrender ourselves implicitly to His guidance! If we could get such a conception of His Divine and glorious character without any blur or modification from old and false ideas, what a delight it would be to think of the Lord! what a joy it would be to worship and serve Him! When we said "Our Father" the whole soul would be upon our lips, the whole heart would be warmed and gladdened, and there would be the impulse of every affection to rush into His arms and to hide ourselves in Him, as it is the impulse of a little child in all its sorrows and in all its joys to be folded in the maternal arms and be drawn to the maternal heart.

This is the form in which the Divine character is revealed to us in the Divine Humanity. It is loving, kind, gentle, patient, considerate of human weakness; it is human; it is touched with a feeling of our infirmities; it sympathizes with us in all our labors and our sorrows, and rejoices in all our joys. Think how the Lord went about doing good when He dwelt with men in a material body; how humble and gentle He was, and how ready to grant any favor! He is the same now in His glorified Humanity. He is our Father, not above the heavens but in the heavens. He is conceivable, accessible, and nigh to every one who calls upon Him, and His name is the synonym and complex of all that is lovely, wise, and good.

2. He teaches us to hallow His name in our lives. We do this when we sincerely desire that those qualities which constitute His Divine character may become finited in us and make us in our degree perfect as our Father in heaven is perfect. Every sincere desire to become transformed into His image and likeness, to become imbued with His spirit; every effort to obey His commandments, and do His will, is a prayer that His name may be hallowed in us. It is a comprehensive petition; it embraces all the qualities of a heavenly character and the means of forming it.

The Lord's name is Jehovah, which denotes His Divine Love. We hallow that name when we receive His love in its own quality and character, without any admixture of the love of the world, without any contamination from the love of self. We hallow it when our motives and purposes accord with His,—and that is when we seek the happiness and the highest good of others. Hallowing this name of the Lord implies a love for all that is good and true and pure; a sincere desire that His love, which flows into our hearts, may flow down into all our affections and pass on to others in the forms of friendship, of social, civil, conjugial, parental love, unchanged from its Divine character, so that in us and through us His love will only be finited and directed to accomplish His infinite purposes.

The Lord's name is God, which denotes the Divine truth. We hallow this name when we desire to hallow the Divine truth, to receive it in its unchanged, unperverted form, without any admixture of human prudence; to make it our light, and our guide, and our way. We hallow the Divine truth when we open our understandings to its reception, as we hallow the light when we open our eyes to receive it. We hallow it when we make our action conform to it, whether it accords with our feelings or not. We hallow the Divine truth when we make it our guide in our business, in society, in politics, in the family, in the relations between husband and wife, parent and child. We hallow the Lord's name just so far as we become the embodiments of all those principles which constitute it,—so far as His love becomes our love, His truth our truth, His purpose our purpose, His way our way.

3. The Sacred Scriptures are His name. The Lord is Divine love and Divine truth. He is the Word. "The Word became flesh and dwelt among men." The Sacred Scriptures are the Word in another form. Therefore our Lord says, "Search the Scriptures, for in them ye think ye have eternal life, and they are they which testify of me." They were given to reveal to men the Divine existence and attributes, and to instruct them concerning the laws and possibilities of their own spiritual nature and the means of obtaining eternal life. They were given in a form adapted to the states of every human mind, from the little child to the highest angel. In its inmost sense, every word relates to the Lord, and expresses in human language some attribute of His nature, some motive and mode of His

action, or some relation to men. However devoid of spiritual and Divine meaning the words may seem to be in the letter, they are the words which the Lord has spoken: " they are spirit and they are life."

We hallow this name of the Lord when we set it apart as distinct from all human compositions; when we regard it as the Word of the Lord and the embodiment of His infinite love and wisdom. We hallow it when we regard it as the Lord speaking to us; when we honestly endeavor to understand what He says, and faithfully to do what He commands. We hallow it when we go to it with docile minds to learn what the Lord teaches, not to confirm our own opinions. We hallow it when we look beneath the surface of the letter and rise above the illusions of appearances into the clear light of spiritual truth, and the eternal verities of spiritual laws. We hallow it in the degree we imbibe its spirit, and make its precepts and commandments the rule of our lives. We hallow it when we regard it as the testimony of a revered and loving Father, who regards us with infinite mercy, to whom we are indebted for all the comforts and blessings we possess, and the power to enjoy them, and whose final purpose in all this is to bless us and make us happy forever. If we hallowed this name according to its worth we should make it our daily study; we should take it for our daily guide in all our labors and enjoyments, and it would be our constant effort to regulate our motives and our actions by its precepts, with the perfect assurance that when we make the law of the Lord the law of our life we are guided by infinite wisdom.

4. The material universe is the Lord's name. " The heavens declare the glory of God, and the firmament show-

eth, His handiwork. Day unto day uttereth speech, and night unto night showeth knowledge. There is no speech nor language where their voice is not heard." How grand and beautiful this name is! The Divine love and wisdom are embodied and expressed in everything the Lord has created. Human science is merely the knowledge of the forms, relations, and qualities of the material universe. Human language is composed of the names we give to the various objects in nature. The objects themselves are the real name of "our Father in the heavens." Sun and moon and star, mountain and ocean, valley and stream, rock and tree, blossom and fruit, insect and fish, bird and animal, in their infinite varieties of character and form are letters and syllables in this great name, and they express each in its own form and use something of the infinite wisdom of Him who created them; they give us some hints of the infinite love of our Heavenly Father.

We hallow this name of the Lord when we see His love and wisdom in the beautiful and useful forms of nature; when the thought passes from the material object to the Divine Creator, and the affections, awakened by the contemplation of such rich profusion and tender, provident care, rise in devout and grateful emotions to their Author. We hallow this glorious and wonderful name when we use all these material objects for the end they were designed. We hallow the beauty of the earth and the grandeur of the heavens when we see in them the beauty and glory of Him who created them; we hallow our food and clothing, and the rich abundance of all things provided for our physical needs, when we use them temperately, wisely, gratefully, to supply our natural wants and preserve a strong and healthy body as the basis for a sound and in-

telligent mind. We hallow this name when we use it to
gain ideas which may become the basis and receptacles
of spiritual truth, and to develop good natural affections
which may become the basis of spiritual affections. We
hallow this name, we set it apart and consecrate it to its
highest and holiest purpose, when we use it as a means
of expressing our love to the neighbor, and our gratitude, our reverence, our obedience, and devotion to the
Lord.

5. Every angel, every man and woman, and every child
is the name of the Lord, so far as they have become the
embodiments of His love and wisdom, and have been created
into His image and likeness. The new-born infant has
capacities in their germs, larger than the material universe,
to become the embodiment of the Divine attributes in
finite forms. Man is the crowning work of the Lord, the
fullest and clearest expression in finite forms of His own
Divine nature. In man He has embodied all the forms
and qualities of the material universe, and He has made
him capable of endless progression.

We hallow this name of the Lord when we look for the
good and true in every human being. We are too prone
to look for the evil and false. We hallow this name when
we respect and love others in the degree that the Lord
" has put His law in their inward parts and has written it
in their hearts." We hallow this name when we do all
in our power to teach those truths and cherish those affections which constitute it. We hallow this name in our
own persons when we regard ourselves as spiritual beings,
when we shun evils as sins against God, when we are diligent in learning spiritual truths, when we cherish heavenly.
affections and day by day, diligently perform the duties

which devolve upon us from love to the neighbor and to the Lord.

These are hints of what is meant by hallowing the Lord's name. Is it not a comprehensive prayer? Is it not full of infinite meanings which touch us on all sides, from within and without? Is it not full of practical wisdom for the guidance of our daily lives? If you have learned to pray in this manner, when you enter the closet and shut the door, even though it may be in a feeble degree, "the Father, who seeth in secret, will reward you openly." Then learn how to offer it. Think it; lisp it; stammer it; work for it; practise it. Put away every evil desire which hinders your asking and reception of its blessing. Ask the Lord to teach you how to say " Hallowed be Thy Name" with the understanding and the heart, and you will find it answered in a clearer knowledge of the Divine wisdom and in a fuller reception of the Divine love. His name will be hallowed in you, and you will become the blessed instrument of hallowing it in others.

# VII.

## THE LORD'S KINGDOM, WHAT IT IS; HOW TO PRAY FOR IT.

*"Thy Kingdom Come."*—Matthew vi. 9.

THE subject to which I invite your attention this morning is one of surpassing grandeur and supreme importance. All earthly kingdoms for whose possession the great men of the earth have studied and labored, and struggled and died, are insignificant in extent and trivial in value compared with the kingdom of our Father in the heavens. Earthly kingdoms rise and fall and pass away: but the Lord's kingdom, when once established, will continue to increase in riches and power and glory forever. There are but few who can gain the possession of an earthly kingdom, and the number who can retain it and enjoy it, is still smaller. But every one can gain a heavenly kingdom who will accept it, and every one who becomes established in it will become endowed with its power, enriched with its treasures, and blessed with its joys more fully forever. No one will ever dispute his royal title, no one will seek or desire to drive him from his throne. But all the good and true on earth and in heaven will unite with the Lord Himself to

107

secure him in his possession, to extend his dominion, and to make his reign enduring, peaceful, and glorious. Such a kingdom is offered to every one of us by the Lord; such a kingdom we are to ask for ourselves and our children; such a kingdom the Lord is in the constant effort to bestow upon us. Let us try to learn its nature and laws, and what we must do to secure its possession.

The petition, "Thy kingdom come," follows in a natural order the one which precedes it. That kingdom can never come to us until we hallow the Lord's name, because it is composed of the principles which constitute the Lord's name, and established by a knowledge and application of them to life. We hallow our Father's name when we worship Him in His Divine Humanity; and we worship Him when we regard the love and wisdom, the order and use of all the Divine forces and principles embodied and revealed to men in the Divine Humanity as sacred and holy, and the only way of gaining eternal life. In the degree we come into this state the Lord's kingdom can come to us. Our hearts are open to welcome it; our understandings gain capacity to receive its light, and power to comprehend its laws and order. The Father's kingdom is composed of the same principles as His name. It is His name organized in form and brought down to man's comprehension and use. The kingdoms of nature are His name written in rock and plant, in the glory of the heavens and the beauty of the earth, in the fowls of the air and the beasts of the field, and in the kingdoms of men. His glorious name is written in clearer lines and more lovely forms in the church on the earth, and the angels in the heavens: but it exists in its infinite perfections only in the Divine Humanity. The questions, however, which specially concern us, at the present time, are, What the Lord's kingdom is, and How we can effectively pray for its coming.

The general conception of a kingdom is that of a number of human beings associated in one government, under one ruler who is called a King. This is a civil kingdom. The kingdom of the Lord is generally and truly regarded as His Church. The members of the Church are His subjects, and taken together, constitute His kingdom upon the earth. To pray for the coming of His kingdom, therefore, is to pray for the extension of His Church. This, in a general sense, is the true idea. But it involves more than we may from a casual observation suppose. The Lord's kingdom does not consist merely of a collection of men and women under one government, but of men and women of a certain character.

A civil kingdom is determined by a natural boundary. All who live within that boundary belong to that kingdom. But in the Lord's kingdom it is not so. All who are external members of the Church do not belong to the Lord's kingdom. It is a kingdom of principles, and citizenship in it is determined by the spiritual principles embodied in the character. Here is an entirely new test of citizenship. The lines which enclose the kingdom and distinguish it from any other are not material or natural, but spiritual. A man may be naturally within the lines and spiritually without them; he may be naturally beyond them and yet spiritually within them.

The true idea of the Lord's kingdom is best illustrated by what are called the kingdoms of nature. All natural substances and objects are divided into the three kingdoms, called mineral, animal, and vegetable. These kingdoms exist together and depend upon each other. You cannot draw a line around any given space and say all within this line is animal, vegetable, or mineral. The lines which divide them are of a very different character. They enter into the forms and qualities of the structure of the individual objects, and the degrees of life which they embody. So it is with men. They belong to the Lord's kingdom who contain its principles and are the spiritual subjects of the Divine government. Before we can intelligently ask for the coming of that kingdom we must have some knowledge of its principles, and it is to this subject your attention is first invited.

The kingdom of our Father in the heavens consists essentially of the Divine love and wisdom as they exist in His Divine Humanity. The Lord rules by the love and wisdom derived from Him. He created human souls in His own likeness and image that they might receive the love and wisdom which flow from Him as light and heat flow from the sun, and thus become His subjects; not the subjects of an arbitrary government, but the subjects of the Divine influences; the subjects whom He created to bless, whom He delights to bless; the subjects of His paternal care and all His providential arrangements. Unlike most human rulers, our Father governs men for their good. His purpose is to bring them into a state in which He can do the most for them, and not to get the most service from them. He is a Father with a heart full of infinite tenderness, and not an exacting tyrant. He seeks to make all the subjects of His government children and not servants, freemen and not slaves; heirs of His power and glory and the riches of His love and wisdom, and not pensioners with a bare pittance. He seeks to establish a kingdom which shall embody His own love and wisdom, be continually enlarging, and whose subjects shall be more and more closely allied to Him and to each other. His kingdom as it exists in its causes and principles in His Divine Humanity consists of all the substances, forms, forces, and qualities that are possible to creative power and to human attainment; it combines all that it is possible for infinite love and wisdom to give, and all that it is possible for created beings to receive.

It is a kingdom of love. It has its origin in the Divine love, which is infinite, and embraces every form which it is possible for love to assume, and every degree which it can attain. It descends to the lowest, it rises to the highest. It may be so weak that it cannot bear a feather's weight, a mere tendency; and it may be so deathless and strong that no force can destroy or resist it. We see the shadow of it even in the material world, in those forces which we call attraction, the bonds by which the material universe is held together. We see it in a little less shadow, in the vegetable kingdom, in those forces which organize each vegetable form, and carry on the processes of creation until it has produced itself in seed. We see it in a little clearer form in the instinct of animals, by which they know their kind, are drawn together in pairs, in flocks and herds, seek the companionship of men, and protect and provide for their offspring.

But we are specially concerned with this kingdom as it is formed and exhibited in man as a spiritual being, for it is the heavenly kingdom for whose coming our Lord taught us to pray. Here we find two distinct degrees of it, the love of love, and the love of truth, or the love of the Lord and the love of the neighbor, celestial love and spiritual love. The love of love is the highest, the inmost, the purest, the most perfect state of existence. It is life, free, full, spontaneous, blissful life. In that state we act from love and love only. We are lifted up and borne onward to the attainment of the highest good in the current of the affections. There is no resistance, there is no failure, there are no obstacles, there are no discords, there is no death. All is life, pure, vivid, peaceful, blissful life.

The second and lower degree of this love is the love of truth, the love of learning it, and of living according to it. This, also, is a pure and heavenly affection. It is the love of knowing what the Divine laws are, for the purpose of regulating the life by them. Those who belong to this kingdom delight to study the Word and the works of the Lord to learn His methods and order of working; and when they have learned a truth they delight to carry it out into all the practical details and relations of life.

These two degrees of the kingdom of love, as they come down into the natural plane of life, assume an indefinite variety of forms, and become the motive forces of all action. They are related to all human activities as heat to the material world, as steam to the engine. Where the love is feeble the action is feeble. Love awakens interest; it gives keenness and power to all the intellectual faculties. We all know how easy it is to do what we love to do. Love lightens labor, and when no obstacles lie in its way life is a holiday and a delight. Look over the wide field of human activities; and you find every man, woman, and child, so far as they are not constrained by necessity, carried along in the current of their affections, and seeking their gratification.

This is true, whatever be the quality of the love, whether good or evil. But the Love which is the life of the Lord's kingdom is holy and good in all its degrees and forms. This is the excellence of it. The more we have of it the

better we are ; the more we give ourselves up to its im-
pulses, and allow ourselves to be carried along in its currents, the higher will be our attainments and the greater
our happiness. The Lord has so constituted us that the
motive force of life, when it is pure, should carry us in the
right direction to attain the highest possibilities of life.

This is the point I wish to make. The underlying, vivifying, and controlling forces of the Lord's kingdom all tend
to righteousness, to human good in its highest form. They
all tend to draw us nearer to Him, and to enlarge our capacities for the reception of life from Him, and to increase
our happiness. They all tend to draw us to each other, to
form us into orderly, harmonious societies ; to make us helpful and a blessing to each other, to make each one a blessing
to all, and all a blessing to each. Where there are no hindrances, as in heaven, this end is attained. The whole kingdom of heaven pours its concentrated life into each member
of it, and every one of its blessed inhabitants gives out its
life to all. Where there are hindrances to a holy and happy
life, as in this world, this Divine force tends to remove them.
It is its tendency, its nature, both in general and particular,
to give to man the largest measures and the highest degrees
of life it is possible for created beings to receive.

The Lord's kingdom in a specific sense is His Divine
truth. Here it is important to get as correct and clear an
idea as possible of what truth really is. " It appears to
man," says Swedenborg, " as if the Divine truth were not
such as to be capable to cause anything to exist, for it is
believed that it is as a voice, which being uttered with the
lips, is instantly dissipated ; but the case is altogether otherwise. The Divine truth proceeding from the Lord is the
veriest reality, and such a reality that all things have existed

8

from it, and subsist by means of it, for whatever proceeds from the Lord is the veriest reality in the universe. Such is the Divine truth, which is called the Word, by which all things were made." We are to conceive of truth not as an abstraction, but as a substance which the Divine love uses to embody itself, and to attain its ends. It is the Divine and spiritual substance out of which the spiritual world and all human souls are formed. Truth is related to love as unorganized matter to those spiritual forces which clothe themselves with it, and mould it into their own forms. It comprises all the laws, order, and arrangement by which the Lord seeks to create a universe of intelligent human beings.

These substances are perfectly adapted in every respect to the nature of the Divine love, and contain within themselves every quality which is essential to make them the perfect instruments of love. Love is life; truth is a substance which yields itself to the plastic forces of life, to be moulded into its form, and to take its perfect impress. Love is spiritual force; truth is perfectly adapted to the reception and transmission of that force to accomplish the ends of love. It is the nature of love to communicate itself, and to conjoin itself to others; it is the nature of truth to receive love, and to be conjoined with it; to become one with it. It is the nature of love to bless, to make others alive with its own happiness; it is the nature of truth to receive life and to be blessed by it, to be the instrument of communicating that blessing to others. Truth is a perfect conductor of love. It is the flesh and bones of love, cast into its own image; married to it, one with it.

Heavenly love, as we have seen, in all its qualities, in its very nature, seeks to give itself to others, to be one with them, to bless them. Truth is a perfect means in the hands of love for accomplishing its purposes. And the two together, in their action and reaction upon each other, are the substances and means which the Lord has created to form His spiritual kingdom in the heavens. Truth comprises all the laws, forms, substances, activities, relations, and modes of operation necessary to carry into full and complete effect the purposes of love ; to display all its qualities ; to communicate all its good.

— The result of the combination and interchange of activities between these two component factors of the Lord's kingdom is the kingdom itself in the form of human beings, who are the embodiments and forms of this love, and the constant recipients and communicators of this life. The Lord's kingdom in the heavens, in its concrete form, is composed of human beings, of angels who were once men, women, and children upon the earth, who are the embodiments of His love and wisdom. As we have seen, there are two elements which enter into the formation of these human beings, which are perfect in themselves and perfectly related to each other. The Lord, therefore, has made the most ample provision for the establishment of this kingdom. It is His sole occupation to establish it, to provide for it, to extend it, to bless it. Everything which He has created, from the least to the greatest, from the lowest to the highest, was created to promote the interests of this kingdom, and has a direct reference to it. Here, then, the Lord directs us to pray for the accomplishment of the purposes for which He lives, and in which He employs His infinite love and wisdom and omnipotent power.

Having endeavored to gain a true idea of what the Lord's kingdom is, and of the principles which compose it, the question naturally arises, How can we effectively pray for its coming? If our prayer is not a hypocritical or a vain prayer, merely an empty sound, the question is equivalent to asking, What can we do to aid in its coming? This is the only question of practical value, and the one to which I desire to call your special attention. It is a kingdom of love. What can we do to bring that love down to earth, and make it the motive power of human action? It is a kingdom of Divine truth. What can we do to bring its light down into the darkness of human error, and make it the guide of human action? It is a kingdom composed of men and women who are becoming the embodiment of the love and wisdom which constitute the Divine character. How can we become the living form of these principles, and the loyal subjects of the King, our Heavenly Father? It is evident that there are many obstacles to the establishment of this kingdom in our own minds, and among men on the earth.

There is a kingdom to subdue and extirpate before the kingdoms of this world can become the kingdoms of our Lord. This kingdom has become established in us, and it must be overthrown. There must be many conflicts and many victories. The theatre of the warfare is not only without but within ourselves. We must be in the daily and constant effort to restrain our selfish and worldly affections. We must lay down our natural, selfish, worldly lives, and take up the cross and follow the Lord. The promised land in which this kingdom is to be established is in the possession of enemies. They must be driven out, and this can only be done " little by little."

This order of procedure is universal. If we desire to build a new house on the site of an old one, the old one must come down. When a farmer desires to raise corn in a field covered with a forest, his first work consists in clearing away whatever cumbers the ground. He must pray for the coming of the new kingdom with his axe and fire and plough. If we desire to have the Lord's kingdom come in our own souls, or in the world, we must clear away the rubbish which preoccupies the ground. If we moved into a house whose windows were covered thick with dust and cob-webs, and we desired to have the kingdom of light come to us, we should not fall upon our knees, and with much solemnity and earnestness cry, O Lord, let thy kingdom of light come into these dark rooms, and into the rooms of every one in the world. We should not continue this prayer from day to day, while we made no effort to remove the obstacles which pre-vented the entrance of the light. If our servant should try to get the light by counting her beads and repeating her Pater-nosters, we should soon teach her a more effective way of praying. We should teach her to pray with brush and water. Why should we not use the same good sense in spiritual things?

We daily repeat the words, "Thy kingdom come." But how can it come to a nature in which there is no room for it? How can it come when the kingdoms of self and the world have full possession? How can purity live with impurity and preserve its sweetness? How can truth dwell with error, discord with harmony, light with dark-ness, health with disease, love with hate, life with death? The first step in becoming the Lord's kingdom, or in establishing it among men, consists in clearing away the obstacles to its coming; it is a destructive, laborious, pain-ful work. This is one reason why we shrink from it, try to content ourselves with repeating words, and seek to take the second step before we have taken the first. We hope to become good before we cease to be evil. But we can never succeed in this way. The kingdom of sin and falsity are first established in us, and that kingdom must be extirpated. Our holy land is filled with enemies who must be put to the sword, whose cities must be levelled with the dust before the Lord can establish His kingdom there. This removal of the obstacles is our work in establishing the Lord's kingdom, and a most important part of it. It is a work that can only be done by us. The Lord does not ask us to create heavenly affections, to originate the principles which constitute His kingdom: He only asks us to receive them. They are of such a nature that they cannot be forced upon us. We must ask for them; we must open our hearts and understandings to receive them. But we cannot receive them passively as an empty vessel receives water. We must take hold of them; we must welcome them. The Lord does not ask the farmer to make his crops grow. His first and essential work consists in preparing the ground. We cannot create light: we can only remove the obstructions to its inflowing. We must shut our door and open the one at which the Lord knocks. If men would pray as sincerely, and wisely, and energetically for spiritual blessings as they do for natural ones, how quickly and largely their prayers would be answered! How rapidly the Lord's kingdom would come to us! Its love would fill the soul with the pure, quickening breath of heaven; its light would stream upon us with noonday brightness; every affection would become vivified by its life, and every thought moulded into its order and loveliness.

This order in the establishment of the Lord's kingdom

applies to our efforts to extend it among men, as well as to
its upbuilding in our own souls. We must first "cast the
beam out of our own eyes before we attempt to cast out the
mote out of our brother's eyes." One of the most effective ways to influence others is to become a centre of influence. Words are not the only means of influence.
Character is more potent than words. When the hearts
of men and women are filled with heavenly love, and their
understandings are radiant with heavenly light, a power
which "makes for righteousness" constantly emanates from
them. They are magnets which attract homogeneous
natures and repel the evil and false. They are a harmo-
nizing and unifying power. An influence flows from them
which tends to quicken into life the germs of good in
others. Their light shines in their deeds. Every word
such a man or woman says is weighted with an influence
greater than the words they utter or the ideas contained in
them. In the degree that the Lord's kingdom comes to
us we shall be the means of its coming to others. We
may see some of the laws which constitute it, and we may
talk about them and commend them, but what we say will
have but little weight with others unless we give to them
the testimony of our lives. Those who pray with their
lives offer the most effective prayer, even though they do
not utter a word. They carry the Lord's kingdom with
them; they are examples of it; they are building it up
while engaged in their business, in their leisure, their recreations, at home or abroad. Let us, then, begin the building of the kingdom in our own minds. Let us seek it first
in all our activities; then our lives will be a constant
prayer for its coming.

The next distinct step in this prayer consists in learning

the laws of this kingdom, all of which are Divine truths. We are not to understand by this that we are to wait until the old kingdom of evil and falsity is destroyed before we begin to learn these laws. The work of destruction and building up must go on together. We must learn truths to discover errors ; to see what to shun and how to shun it. We need truths as weapons to combat our evils. Truth is a sword, a shield, a wall of defence. We cannot meet the assaults of our spiritual enemies and overcome them without it. But no truth becomes ours until it is applied to life; and we cannot apply it to life until we begin to shun evils and false principles as sins against God.

The Lord has given us in the Sacred Scriptures a full code of the laws of citizenship in His kingdom, illustrated by innumerable examples. They are so plainly stated that a child can understand their essential principles. They are all summed up in the Golden Rule, to do to others as we would have them do to us. They are more distinctly and particularly stated in the Ten Commandments, and they are unfolded in an endless variety of forms, in statutes and precepts, and specially illustrated and enforced by the example of our Lord Himself. We must learn these laws for the purpose of knowing what to do to become members of this kingdom and to aid others in doing the same thing.

These laws are not theories, or speculations, or doctrines to be received by faith, with the idea that there is any virtue in a merely intellectual knowledge of them. One of the greatest hindrances to the coming of the Lord's kingdom, even among those who study its laws, is that they do not learn them for the purpose of knowing what to do so much as what to think. But the law of life is the same in spiritual as in natural things. If we desired to become citizens of an earthly kingdom, we should seek to know what steps to take with the purpose of taking them. Our knowledge would be of no use to us unless we acted according to it. A kingdom cannot be established by abstract laws. The law only points out the way to secure the end. We must use the same practical good sense in spiritual that we do in natural things. The Lord has taught us to pray that His kingdom may come. We know that it is the purpose of His love to establish His kingdom on the earth. If we desire to become citizens of that kingdom we must learn its laws.

The next and final step consists in doing what they require. If they only required a formal assent to them, the work could be quickly and easily accomplished. But we must not only assent to the laws, we must become their embodiment. The law must be put in our inward parts, and written in our hearts. The kingdom of God is within us, and only as it is established within us can we become members of it. Love to the Lord and the neighbor must become the ruling motives of our lives. Our understandings must become the recipients of Divine truth, and our lives must be employed in some kind of useful service. By exercising heavenly affections and doing heavenly work the Lord's kingdom will gradually become established within us, we shall become members of it, and our whole nature will be transformed into the image and likeness of the Lord.

There is no higher honor and no greater good possible to created beings than to become members of the Lord's kingdom. The King of kings and Lord of lords does not regard the members of His kingdom as subjects, but as children. The King is our Father, and He desires to. have us partake of His nature, bear the beauty and loveliness of our parentage, and become heirs of His riches, power, glory, and blessedness. Such is the nature of spiritual power and riches that they are not diminished by division. Our Father can give to all His children as much and even more than He could if there was only one. As the numbers of His kingdom increase, the portion which every one will receive will be enlarged and multiplied. We have every conceivable motive to offer this petition in word and deed. In His Divine Providence the Lord has supplied us with the most abundant means and opportunities to co-operate with Him, and with all the good and true on earth and in heaven in establishing His kingdom. Let us be diligent and faithful in removing all the obstacles in ourselves and in others to its coming; let us be earnest and docile in learning its laws, and scrupulous in regulating our thoughts and in living according to them. Then His kingdom will come to us, we shall become citizens of it, and partakers of its power and glory, its peace and rest.

# VIII.

## DOING THE LORD'S WILL IN THE EARTH AS IN HEAVEN.

———•———

"*Thy will be done in earth as it is in heaven.*"—Matt.
vi. 10.

THIS clause of the Divine Prayer, short and simple as
it is, reveals the Lord's purposes in the creation of the
material universe, and in all the operations of His Divine
Providence. The Lord created the material universe to
be the basis of His spiritual universe. The heavens rest
upon the earth as the mind upon the body. Earth is the
seminary of heaven. The creation of human beings who
are to people the heavens, takes place upon the earth.
All distinct and permanent creation is in ultimates. This
is so, not only in general, but in particular. We all acknowledge that the beginning of our existence takes place
in this world, in the earth. It is equally true that every
spiritual faculty which we shall possess, every affection we
shall ever exercise and enjoy, and every idea we shall
gain through the coming eternity, has its beginning in the
earth. We gain the materials here, the germs are cre-

ated here. They will blossom and bear fruit and be indefinitely multiplied and perfected to eternity. But only those principles will be perfected which are implanted here. It follows as a necessary consequence that the broader we lay the foundation, and the greater the variety of truths we learn and of the affections we exercise, and the more excellent their quality, the greater room there will be for increase and perfection in the spiritual world.

There are three distinct and complete degrees of the human mind, natural, spiritual, and celestial, just as in every seed there are the germs of leaves, blossoms, and fruit; only in man these degrees of life are more complete and distinct. The two higher degrees, the spiritual and the celestial, may be opened, and they may not. If they are ever opened the beginning of the process must be made while we are on the earth. If only the natural degree is opened we shall live in that plane of our faculties forever. If the beginning of a genuine spiritual life is made here, we shall rise to that plane and live in it, acquiring its truths and enjoying its blessings. If the celestial degree of the mind is opened we shall live in the highest heaven and enjoy the sweetest peace and the deepest blessedness it is possible for finite beings to attain. In the degree that we lay the foundations for doing the will of the Lord on the earth shall we continue to do it in the heavens. This is the law of relation between this life and the life to come.

The organization of the material body before our birth bears the same relations to its capacities to see, hear, receive sensations, and perform the functions of a human being in this world that the spiritual body, while clothed in the garments of flesh, bears to its capacities to know, love, and enjoy when it is raised up into the spiritual world. As spiritual beings we are in an embryonic state while we dwell in the earth of the material body. If a child is born into this world without eyes there is no way in which it can be endowed with the power of seeing. According to the same law, when we are born into the spiritual world by resurrection from the material body, we can only see, hear, and gain a consciousness of those spiritual objects, and love, know, and enjoy other beings and things in the form and according to the degree and capacity of the spiritual organs which were formed in the earth. There is, therefore, a principle of momentous importance involved in this clause of the Lord's Prayer. When we offer it, we pray for our eternal future ; we pray that the beginnings of an immortal life may be made here, and that these beginnings may be the germs of capacities for the varied, rich, and complete happiness of heaven. There are a few obvious inquiries which we need to make to bring the subject clearly before us.

We must first get a clear idea of what is the will of the Lord in heaven. It is His will, His purpose, that men may have eternal life. He created man for the express purpose of blessing him. The Lord's will is His love, and it is the nature of heavenly love to give all its own to be another's. It is the essential nature of the Divine character to bless, to give itself in as large measures and perfect quality as possible. This is the purpose for which everything in the universe was created. Everything, from the least to the greatest, is exactly adapted to this end. The Lord could not create a finite form better adapted to receive His love and wisdom, and be blessed by them, than the human. Man can receive the Divine love and wisdom in their highest finite forms, and there is nc assignable limit to his capacity to receive and enjoy. It is the Lord's will that every human being should receive the largest possible measures of happiness. There is nothing too great, or too beautiful, or too good for the Lord to give.

It is His will, also, to make it cost us as little as possible. He desires to give us the most for the least. In this respect His will is directly the reverse of selfish men. They desire to get the most for the least. The Lord desires to give the most for the least.. He desires to have us get the highest good in the easiest way. He is so desirous of this, that He helps us all He can : He came into the world to point out the way, to be the way. "This is the will of the Father, that every one who seeth the Son, and believeth in Him, may have eternal life." The Lord does not exact the least thing of us which is not essential to the attainment of the end.

I do not know of anything in which men who claim to be Christians have more misunderstood the Lord's character and purpose than in His infinite desire and effort to give the largest and richest good to His children. It is the common opinion that the Lord is " a hard master, reaping where he has not sowed." But this is an entire mistake. If He asks us to deny ourselves, it is because His will cannot be done in us until we make room for the operations of His spirit. If He commands us to pluck out the right eye if it offends us, it is because it blinds us to something far more beautiful than can be seen by our natural sight. So it is in every case. He never asks us for any self-denial except for the purpose of doing us a good which He could not give us without it. He never takes anything from us, or permits anything to be taken from us, except for the purpose of giving us a greater good in its place. What a comfort it would be if we could keep this truth clearly before us, in our daily labors and trials : " The Lord is seeking to give me the highest good I can receive, and if He takes anything away it is to make room for it."

It is the Lord's will that we should live according to the commandments, shunning what they forbid, and doing what they enjoin, because they are laws of life, because they are the paths which lead to life, and any deviation from them is the way to death. The Lord did not give the commandments to men because He desired to lay any restrictions upon them. He did it to point out the way to the attainment of the highest good. When we obey them we follow the directions of infinite wisdom. The Lord teaches us to pray that His will may be done in the earth as it is in heaven. The next question which it is important to know is, How is His will done in heaven ? We can only mention some of the general principles which regulate the life there.

In heaven they keep the commandments, the first of which is, " Thou shalt love the Lord thy God with all thy heart." The heavenly inhabitants do this. Their hearts are open to the Lord, and their faces are turned towards Him. This love is not a mere sentiment, an impulse of the affections ; it is a principle, a rule of life. The test of it is not an outburst of passionate emotion, breaking forth into song. " He that hath My commandments, and keepeth them, he it is that loveth Me." The Lord has not one rule of life for heaven, and another for the earth. Life, according to the commandments, is heaven, and when men keep them as well as the angels it will be heaven upon the earth. All the angels love the Lord in the degree that their affections were opened in this world. Some love Him in a celestial way, some in a spiritual degree, and some in a natural. The power to love differs in every one. They love Him with all their hearts ; but some hearts are much larger than others. Their love manifests itself in keeping His commandments. Those in the first heaven keep them from the love of obedience ; those in the second heaven from the love of the truth. They see that they are laws of life; they see their beauty, harmony, order, and they love to carry them out in all their relations to each other. Those who dwell in the highest heaven do them unconsciously and spontaneously. These laws are engraved upon their hearts, the celestial inhabitants are the forms of these laws, and all their activities flow according to their harmonies. They keep them just as the tree keeps them when it blossoms and bears fruit. Their affections and thoughts flow in the currents of the Divine order, and their whole being is filled with light, love, and blessedness.

The second great law of heaven, and the way the Lord's will is done there is, the inhabitants love one another. Some love others as themselves ; others more than themselves. This love also is something more than a sentiment ; it is *done.* It is carried out into all the relations of life. They do all they can to help each other, to make each other happy. We cannot conceive of an angel being envious, or jealous, or unkind, of bearing false witness, or of finding fault with his fellows. We cannot conceive of an angel coveting another's place or possessions, or of neglecting the uses of his own to criticise the work of another. Every one loves to be in his own place, and to do his own work in the best manner he can, and in everything he does he has primary regard to the good of others.

As a result of this love for the Lord and the neighbor, there is perfect harmony in all the domestic, social, civil, and spiritual relations of the heavenly inhabitants. Each one is living for all. The whole heaven is giving its service to each one of its inhabitants. How lovely and beautiful those relations must be! The feelings are kind, the speech is pure and gentle, the sympathies are warm and sensitive, the hands are gentle and strong to help. The only ambition to be great is to serve. Every one is in his place, desires to be in his place, does that which he can do best, and loves to do it.

Heaven is a society of human beings associated together according to mutual tastes and character. Those who love each other the best, who are of homogeneous natures, and consequently can be of the greatest service to each other, live in the most intimate relations. Supreme love to the Lord and unselfish love of the neighbor are the governing principles of action, and these principles are carried into all the details of life. That is the way the Lord's will is done in the heavens.

It is also done in another way. It is the Lord's will that every human being should have everything which will promote his happiness in the fullest and highest degree. The inhabitants of heaven possess everything necessary to their happiness. Their clothing, habitation, climate, situation equal the highest ideals of every one in every particular. The blessed inhabitants cannot ask for anything which the Lord will not give them. The promise which our Lord made to His disciples is perfectly

9

fulfilled. "If ye shall ask anything in my name, I will do it." There is nothing to disturb, annoy, offend ; everything to comfort, satisfy, and bless.

The Lord teaches us to pray that His will may be done in the earth as it is in heaven. The earth, as it is used in the Word, has large and various meanings. And the Lord desires to have His will done in it in every sense. By earth, in its lowest sense, we are to understand the material world. The Lord seeks to have His will done in it as it is in the heavens. He seeks to have it perfectly adapted to man's condition while he lives in the material body. He created it to be our home in the infancy of our being, and He has supplied it with all the materials necessary for our food and clothing and habitation. How beautiful and grand He has made it ! How richly He has supplied it with everything which is conducive to our comfort and pleasure! Look at His provisions for one want,— food for the growth and sustenance of the material body ! What an infinite variety ! How delicious it is ! How nicely adapted to all tastes, and to the upbuilding of the whole physical structure ! In what beautiful forms He presents it to us ! How attractive He makes every step of the process of its preparation ! Take one fruit as an example,—the apple. The tree itself is beautiful, and stretches out its motherly arms near the earth as if handing its blessings down to us. The leaves are beautiful, and what a glory of blossoms crowns the tree ! How delicate and lovely their crimson tints ! How, pure as an angel's smile, they open their lips, whose speech is fragrance, filling the whole air with its sweetness. The old orchards I roamed in when a boy ! They smile on me yet. I feel their benedictions now. I did not think then that they were doing it in obedience to the Divine will; but I see it now, and I shall see it more and more clearly forever.

When this rich dower of beauty and fragrance has served its use in introducing and cherishing the tender germs of the fruit it passes away, and the old arms gradually bend towards the earth with the increasing weight of their precious burden. How lovely in form and color the fruit! How delicious to the keen appetite its taste! How much comfort and pleasure and sustenance it supplies! I did not see the Lord's goodness in this bounty then; but I see it now, and the lovely pictures of His working for me when I knew it not fill my heart with gratitude to-day! This is one example of the many ways in which the Lord is expressing His love, is doing His will in the earth as it is in the heavens. I know that no earthly trees or earthly fruits can compare with those which blossom and bear fruit in the paradise above. But they are adapted to our states in this world. They supply our present wants, and they are the best the Lord can do for us with such rough materials.

But He can do better for us the more earnestly and intelligibly we pray to Him to do it. Here we may see the true use and nature of prayer. It is a well-known fact that all fruits have been much improved in size and flavor by culture. The varieties and abundance have also been much increased. So great has this improvement been, that we should regard our most delicious fruits as hardly fit to eat in their wild, primitive state. How have they been changed? By prayer! By the only effectual prayer. Men have prayed with the plough and the hoe, and the pruning-hook. They studied the

Divine commandments written in the soil and in the climate, and in the sun and winds, and in the plant itself. They studied diligently to discover what the plant loved, what materials it could use to the best advantage, and as fast as they discovered these laws they kept them. They prayed for a better and more abundant fruit, and they prayed in the right way ; and their prayers were answered.

The Lord is doing His will on the earth as it is done in heaven in a larger and different way from what is generally supposed. The material universe, and every useful and beautiful material object is cast into the mould of heavenly forms. There are three kingdoms in nature because there are three kingdoms in the spiritual world to which the material kingdoms correspond. They are the effects of spiritual causes. There are minerals, plants, birds, and animals on the earth because there are minerals and plants, birds and animals in heaven. The Lord is carrying the great purposes of His love into effect according to the same laws, and by the same means in the earth as He does in heaven. He creates the same objects that they may perform the same use to men in the material body that they do on a higher plane to human beings in a spiritual body. The earth and all material objects are shadows of the spiritual earth which we shall inhabit when we have served our apprenticeship here, and the material objects in their various forms of mineral, plant, and animal are only the rough casts and rude outlines of corresponding spiritual objects in heaven. When we pass from earth to heaven, we shall not pass from the known to the entirely unknown. We shall find the same objects in general that we have left behind us. The difference will not consist in unlikeness and opposites, but in greater variety, in surpassing beauty and grandeur, in supreme excellence in quality, and in a more complete adaptation to every human condition.

The Lord is doing His will on the earth as He is doing it in heaven. When we study science, and learn the laws, forces, qualities, and relations of one object to another, we are learning how the Lord accomplishes His will, what means He employs, and in what form His will becomes embodied. We find also that He employs human agency. He does the best He can by working from within according to general laws to give man food, clothing, and habitation. But to carry out His purposes of good to man in the most complete manner He needs our co-operation. By working through us He can obtain better results than He can by working through nature alone. He takes His children into partnership, gives them abundant materials, and teaches them how to use them, to improve them. He teaches us how to be creators, and gives us opportunities to work for others, and do good to them, as He works for and blesses us. By these means the affections are enlarged, and all our intellectual and spiritual faculties are developed. The Lord desires to have all His children well fed, well clothed, to have them dwell in comfortable and beautiful habitations on the earth as well as in heaven. For this end He works, for this end He desires to have us work with Him.

The Lord desires to have His children live in domestic comfort, love, and peace. Those who are trying to bring their own families into this condition are offering this prayer. When husband and wife tenderly and truly respect and love one another, and seek each others' happiness; when children love their parents, and are obedient

to them, and try to make them happy; when they love and
respect each other, and try to serve each other; when all
the members of a family combine to live for each other,
according to the measure of their success, they are doing
the Lord's will on the earth as it is done in the heavens.
They are praying for it without ceasing, and their prayer
is answered. The same principle applies to all the social,
civil, and industrial relations of men. Every man and
every woman who is trying to improve the condition of
humanity in this world is offering this prayer, and is doing it in the only way in which the Lord can answer it.
Oh, that the prayers of men were more fervent, and more
intelligent, and more constant! It is a blessed sign, full
of promise, that men's prayers are coming down from the
abstract and ideal into the practical and real.

But we pass on to notice another meaning of earth,
which has a most important bearing upon our personal
happiness and excellence. By the earth is meant the
natural mind which is the subject of all our natural
thoughts, desires, passions, and attainments. In this petition the Lord teaches us to ask that His will may be
done in the natural degree of our life as it is in the spiritual. The spiritual degree of the mind is first regenerated. We learn spiritual truth which teaches us how we
ought to live. We have aspirations after a heavenly life.
We resolve to live it and we make efforts to do it. It is
not difficult to acknowledge the beauty and excellence of
a heavenly life, and when the passions are at rest and we
are not exposed to temptations, to dream of living it.

But when we bring these heavenly principles of supreme
love to the Lord and equal love to the neighbor down into
natural affection, thought, and deed, we find they come

into conflict with all our selfish and worldly desires, and a long and weary conflict must be waged before the heavenly gains full lodgement in the earthly, subdues its obduracy, moulds it into its own likeness, and moves it to harmony with itself. The Lord teaches us to pray that all our natural affections may be clarified into heavenly purity; that a heavenly love may imbue and control our natural wills; that heavenly light may illuminate our understandings; that heavenly kindness and gentleness may characterize all our actions; that our speech may be gentle, and true, and helpful, and all our actions useful and good.

When we are trying to bring heaven down into the earth; when we are learning the truth; when we are performing some use, from love to others, we are offering this petition continually. Husband and wife are praying this prayer when they are living a true married life. The merchant, and the mechanic, and the seamstress, and the teacher; the cook, and the mistress of a household; the lawyer, and the physician, and the minister, and every one in any useful office is offering this prayer who is working from love to others. He is translating it into deeds; is working for the accomplishment of the Lord's will both in himself and in others, and just so far as he offers it fervently, patiently, persistently, it will be answered.

We must not expect the whole work to be done instantly. The farmer does not expect an immediate answer when he prays to have a harvest of wheat where there is a forest of giant trees. He must pray long with his axe, with fire, with ploughshare driven through the hard earth, with seed cast into the ground. Then he must wait for the Lord to come with light and warmth, with rain and dew, before he can see His will accomplished. So must we diligently pray, and faithfully labor, and patiently wait for the coming of His spiritual kingdom into our own hearts and understandings. It is a great work, and we must pray without ceasing and faint not. If we do, our prayer will be answered. The natural and the spiritual mind will become one. The Lord's will will be done on the earth in us as it is in the heavens within us. But we must not forget that we never offer this prayer, however often we may repeat the words, until we try to do it.

By earth is also signified the Church in the world. Here we might expect to find the Lord's will done as it is in heaven. Its members profess to be followers of the Lord, to believe in His Word, and to live a heavenly life. But it is often difficult to discover in the societies of the Church any similarity to the societies in heaven except in form. We do not find the great law of love to be the controlling principle of action. We do find bigotry, pride, hypocrisy, hatred, love of self and the world, ignorance of heavenly laws, and indifference to them. In business, in social and civil life, in the privacy of home, and in public affairs, it is difficult to distinguish the members of the Church from those who make no profession of religion. But our Lord teaches us to pray that the earthly society may be animated by the same spirit, guided by the same principles, and engaged in the same work as the heavenly societies. They have the same Father; they are members of the same family; heirs to the same inheritance. They only dwell in different provinces of the same kingdom. As the earth is the ground in which the heavenly seed is planted and the germs of heavenly blessings take root, we must be diligent in planting, faithful in cultivating and protecting them. Every genuine member of the Lord's kingdom is an embodiment of a heavenly force and a medium of transmitting it. We stand between heaven and the society to which we belong. We communicate what we are ; and the character of every society is the sum of the intelligence, energy, love, order, purity, and devotion its members contribute to it. Let us who are members of this society pray this prayer, and constantly, patiently, and faithfully labor to make it a vigorous and thriving branch of the Lord's kingdom.

There is much thought and said in the Church about going to heaven. Wearied with the labors and contradictions of this life, tormented by its cares, disappointed by its illusions and unsatisfying joys, we long for the freedom and rest, the joys and peace of heaven, which we hope to gain only by escaping from the world. But our Lord teaches us to pray that His will may be done in the earth as it is in heaven. He reverses the order of our purposes. We are to aim and to labor to bring heaven down to earth ; to make every society a heavenly society. It is not by escaping from the labor, but by putting a heavenly purpose into it and giving it a heavenly direction ; it is not by withdrawing from societies and withholding our hands and closing our hearts to its work, that we can gain heaven here or hereafter, but by bringing the principles of heaven into our work and worship ; by uniting with others and extending our influence as widely as possible. It should be our aim and our constant effort, as far as lies in our power, to make this society a living, vigorous member of the Lord's kingdom. We should seek to make ourselves a medium of transmitting the principles, the light, the order, the harmony, the purity, the vital power, and the peace of heaven to the whole body of the society.

The essential principle of heaven is love to the Lord.

Let us try to bring this law of a heavenly life into all our relations with one another as members of a society of the Lord's kingdom.    Let us desire and labor that His will, not ours, except so far as it coincides with it, may be done in our society; that His way may be our way, His purpose our purpose.    May we look to Him, keep the door of our hearts open to Him, that He may guide us by His wisdom, vivify us by His love, and make us willing instruments in His hands of doing His will and helping others to do it.

The members of the Lord's kingdom in heaven love one another with an unselfish and devoted affection.    Let us bring this love into all our relations with one another.    Let us feel kindly towards all.    Let us give to every one all the aid we can in overcoming evil, learning truth, and living a heavenly life.    Then we shall pray this prayer without ceasing.    Every aspiration will ascend as incense to the Lord, and will return to us as a purer love, a clearer light, and a larger capacity to do His will; and through us, according to the measure of our ability, we shall become a society which is a branch of the heavenly kingdom, and which is doing the Lord's will upon the earth as it is done in heaven.

# IX

# DAILY BREAD: WHAT IT IS: HOW TO PRAY FOR IT.

---

*"Give us this day our daily bread."*—Matt. vi. 11.

In every prayer something is involved of far more value to us as spiritual beings than the special good we seek. All asking implies dependence upon others for the help we desire, and in this acknowledgment of our dependence upon others for aid in supporting life and gaining its highest blessings lies one of the essential conditions of human progress. Human brotherhood, and all the blessings of industrial, social, civil, and domestic life grow out of this interdependence of one human being upon another. If we had no need of one another, if we could do nothing for one another, human society could not exist. There could be no more intercourse between human beings than there is between one stone and another. All the activities, uses, and delights of human society grow out of human wants. The knowledge and acknowledgment of our dependence upon the Lord for life and all its bless-

139

ings is still more important. In the degree we feel it we shall constantly look to Him and seek to come into such relations with Him that He can give and we can receive the blessings we need. Unless we acknowledge Him; unless we feel some want and know that He has the power and the disposition to supply it, we shall not go to Him. For this reason He is in the constant effort to reveal Himself to us, to bring us into such relations with Him that we can ask and receive what we need. When we really feel our dependence upon the Lord and understand His willingness to bestow upon us the highest good we can receive, we shall go to Him, and our asking will not be a hypocritical or a vain prayer. It will be sincere, ardent, and earnest.

All the preceding petitions of this Divine prayer lead up to the one we are considering. They are natural and orderly steps to it. When we know the Lord as our Father in the heavens, kind, loving, tender, and watchful over His children, and ready to abundantly supply us with all we need; when we are disposed to hallow His name by regarding all the attributes of His nature as pure and holy, as love and wisdom themselves; when from this knowledge of the Lord's nature we desire to have His kingdom established in us, and His will done in us in all our natural affections, thoughts, and activities, then we come into a state in which we see and delight to feel our dependence upon the Lord. We begin to see something of the beauty and perfection of the Divine character, and we desire to obtain the means of growing into the likeness and image of our Heavenly Father. We desire to be sustained, guided, fed by Him. We feel our need of His support, and we can sincerely and humbly ask Him to give us our daily bread. Every sincere prayer is the voice of a want: it is the want speaking. If we pray to our Heavenly Father, it is an acknowledgment of our dependence upon Him, and of our belief that He can help us. The faith may be weak, but it is strong enough to lead us to ask. The Lord teaches us to ask Him for our daily bread. Let us consider what is meant by daily bread; why we should ask for it; how we should ask; and what will be the effects of receiving it.

I. What are we to understand by bread? Every child knows its specific and natural meaning. But it is something more than the specific substance we call bread. It is a general term embracing all food of all kinds. It comprises every substance which appeases hunger and supplies materials to repair the ever-wasting tissues of the body. When we pray for bread, then, we ask the Lord for natural food of all kinds for the supply of our natural wants. But why should we ask the Lord to give us what He is constantly providing in some measure, whether we ask Him or not? Those who deny His existence have as rich and varied an abundance of food as the most devout. All food products grow according to immutable laws. Prayer does not strengthen or weaken or change the law. The Lord gives no special favors to the good in this respect. " He maketh His sun to rise on the evil and on the good, and sendeth His rain on the just and the unjust." The Lord provides for every living thing. " Behold the fowls of the air," He says, " for they sow not, neither do they reap nor gather into barns; yet your Heavenly Father feedeth them." Why should we ask Him to do what He is doing? Because by asking we acknowledge that we are dependent upon Him for our bread by whatever agencies

He sends it to us.   Our Heavenly Father feeds the fowls of the air and the beasts of the field; He clothes the lily with beauty, and makes the hills and valleys smile with harvests.   The fact that He gives to all creatures their food according to a universal law, does not detract in the least from His agency in making the provision. Natural law is simply His wise way of giving us our daily bread.   Human agency in producing fruits and food does not diminish His providence in their creation.   He gives us the privilege of co-operating with Him for our own culture and pleasure; but all our power to do it is momentarily derived from Him.   Our food of every kind is as truly and as fully the Lord's gift as it would be if He placed it upon our table at every meal.

But our agency in procuring our bread hides from us the Lord's providence and working.   We attribute to the universal laws according to which the Lord works the creative power.   We mistake the instrument or method for the Being who employs it.   In this way we are led to forget and deny the Lord and trust to ourselves alone, and to live only a natural life.   But our Heavenly Father desires to have us know Him "whom to know aright is life everlasting."   He desires to have us see His goodness and mercy, His love and wisdom, in all the provisions He has made for our natural good, for our protection and the supply of all our material wants.   He desires to win our love that He may open the interior planes of our minds, and come to us and bestow upon us larger and more precious spiritual blessings.   It is not for Himself that He asks us to pray to Him or desires to have us acknowledge Him, but for our own good.   In the degree He can get us to look up to Him and open our hearts to Him, He can bless us. If we regarded our food as a daily gift from the Lord, we should not eat it as the animal does; our thoughts would rise to the Lord at every meal, and our hearts would be filled with gratitude for His provident and loving care. Every morsel of food would have a more precious value than its power to supply a natural want; it would lead us to know and love our Heavenly Father, and to become more fully His children.

How shall we pray for our daily bread? Not alone in words. We cannot get it in that way, because the Lord cannot give it to us in that way except in a most meagre and imperfect manner. One of the conditions of a full and varied supply is wanting. He has made our co-operation necessary in gaining our bread. We cannot do much; but the little is one link in the chain of causes by which the end is accomplished. We must, therefore, do our part. We must prepare the ground, cast the seed into it, protect the growing plants from harm, cultivate them, and gather the harvest when it is ripe. The most devout and persistent urgency of words, the most rigid formalities would not procure a morsel of bread for us. The husbandman knows how to worship, and what sacrifices to offer that will be efficacious in filling his granaries and loading his table with food. But while he is doing his work and in doing it, he should acknowledge that all his labor would be vain without the Lord's co-operation; he should be in the constant acknowledgment of his dependence upon Him. He should feel his absolute dependence upon his Heavenly Father for these precious gifts. He should pray without ceasing and with perfect faith, "Give us this day our daily bread." If we worked in this frame of mind, we should be living near the Lord;

we should be in constant communion with Him while engaged in our daily employments, and our hearts would overflow with gratitude and praise. Our prayer, also, would be answered because it would be offered in His name; that is, according to the laws of His Divine order. If all men prayed in this spirit and worked in this way there would be no want. The Lord would bless their basket and their store.

II. But man has a higher plane of faculties than the animal, and he needs bread of a corresponding excellence. By bread we are to understand all the substances which support and nourish his spiritual nature. All consciousness of life is gained by organization. The spirit is an organic form as well as the body. It is a spiritual body subject to spiritual laws. A mental, or spiritual faculty is a spiritual organ, in the same sense as a material faculty is a material organ. The faculty of seeing is the eye; of hearing, the ear; of feeling, the nerves of sensation. The faculty of knowing, of thinking, of loving, are spiritual organs. They have their origin, their laws of development, the substances of which they are formed. They must have their daily bread. " Man doth not live by bread only, but by every word that proceedeth out of the mouth of the Lord doth man live."

The spirit is the real man in every respect. It is in the human form. The material body is cast into its mould. It is organized within and without, in every least and greatest part, as the material body. It has bones, arteries, veins, nerves, flesh and blood, heart and lungs, eyes and ears, and every organ necessary to perform all the functions of a human being. But the substances of which they are formed are spiritual, and as distinct from matter as the mind is distinct from the body, and as superior to it as love and knowledge are superior to heat and light. This spiritual organism requires food to supply its wastes and to develop its powers. The organic forms of the material body are constantly wasting away, and must be constantly supplied with food to repair the waste. The same process in principle is going on in the spiritual body. The forces which operate upon it from within and without dissipate its substance, and would destroy if the waste was not supplied and the organization constantly renewed.

This analogy between the material and the spiritual bodies gives force, a distinct, literal, and comprehensible meaning to many passages in the Sacred Scriptures which have been regarded as figurative and to have only a vague and inferential application to practical life. When our Lord says, "I have meat to eat that ye know not of," "My meat is to do the will of Him that sent me and to finish His work," He reveals a great law of universal application: He states a Divine fact. His human nature, or the human plane of His being with which He clothed His Divine nature and with which He identifies Himself, did receive its existence, its growth, its support, and all its power from the essential Divine within Him which He constantly refers to as the Father. Life, which is substance itself, was constantly supplied from the uncreated fountain within. When He says, "The Father that dwelleth within me, He doeth the works," He states a literal truth, applicable to His human nature before it was glorified or made Divine. He assumed it to make it a medium of communicating His Divine life to men in forms which they could receive and appropriate. Therefore He calls

10

Himself "the bread of life," and declares that we must eat His flesh and drink His blood. "I am the living bread," He says, "which came down from heaven; if any man eat of this bread he shall live forever, and the bread that I will give is my flesh, which I will give for the life of the world." "Whoso eateth my flesh and drinketh my blood hath eternal life." He does not mean by these words that He is going to suffer vicariously for man, and by that means save him from spiritual death. He means just what He says. He is the bread that came down from heaven, He is the living water which becomes in those who drink it "a well of water springing up unto everlasting life." The life which constantly flows from Him is a substance which bears the same relation to the spiritual body that natural • bread bears to the material body, and renders it the same service. In perfect accordance with this plain statement of our Lord, Swedenborg says, "The life of angels and spirits is not supported by any food like that of this world, but by every word which comes forth from the mouth of the Lord, as the Lord Himself teaches when He says, ' Man shall not live by bread alone, but by every word that proceedeth out of the mouth of God.' The fact is that the Lord alone is the life of all. From Him come all and everything which angels and spirits think, speak, and do. Thus the universal heaven and the universal world of spirits live by everything which proceeds out of the mouth of the Lord, and every one has thence his life; nay, this is the case not only with the heaven and the world of spirits, but also with the whole race of mankind. If angels, spirits, and men were deprived of this *meat* they would instantly expire."

By the words which proceed out of the mouth of the
Lord we are not to understand mere verbal expressions,
but those Divine and substantial forces of love and truth
which constantly flow from Him, and which are to all
spiritual life as the heat and light of the sun to vegetable
life.

One of the great difficulties in understanding this subject consists in our utterly inadequate and false notions
concerning love and truth. Love is regarded as a feeling
and truth as a matter of words, when in reality love is the
cause of all feeling and of all the activities of life; and
truth is the veriest reality and substantial existence in the
universe. Words are only the signs or names of truths.
Love and truth are the substances from which all things are
derived, and out of which they are created. God *is* love.
Love is His flesh, the bread with which He feeds all intelligent beings. His blood is Divine truth, which cleanses
from sin the soul that drinks it; truth sustains, enlarges,
invigorates, and builds up the human soul. Truth is the
blood of the spiritual body, and carries in its red currents the substances of which it is organized. It is real,
genuine, substantial drink. With regard to this subject
Swedenborg, speaking of man's nature and quality, says,
" His spirit is greatly delighted with knowledge, insomuch
that it seems of all things the most desirable; it is his
food whereby he is refreshed, as is the external man by
terrestrial food. This food, which is that of the spirit, is
communicated to his external man, to the end that the external man may be adapted to the internal. But the different kinds of food succeed each other according to the
following order: celestial food is every good principle of
love and charity from the Lord; spiritual food is every

truth of faith. On these kinds of food the angels live. From these exists a food, which is also celestial and spiritual, but of an inferior angelic nature, on which live angelic spirits. From this again exists a food, celestial and spiritual, still inferior, which is that of reason and of science thence derived. On this live good spirits. Lastly comes corporeal food, which is proper to man while he lives in the body. These kinds of food correspond with each other in a wonderful manner."

It is not, therefore, a figure of speech which our Lord uses when He calls Himself the "bread of life." He states a universal fact. Every substance which gives and sustains life is a form of His love and wisdom in that plane of the creation in which it exists. The harvests of wheat and corn which clothe our prairies and cover our hills; the delicious fruits which nestle among the leaves, hang in purple clusters from the vine, and load the trees with their precious burdens, embodying odors and savors and substances for the sustenance and delight of man, are all forms, each after its own kind, of the Lord's love and truth. The loaf of bread upon our table is the Divine love in material form and substance as truly as those forces which kindle into holy ardor the affections of the angels. We know from our own experience that love gives us strength, excites to action, and sustains us in the most protracted labors of body and mind. We know that there is no thought and no action where love is wanting. The Divine love, which is life, sustains; power is the bread we are to daily ask the Lord to give us. How are we to ask?

1. By repeating the words the Lord has given us. There is a great and precious use in regular, stated prayer.

Our children should learn this prayer and form the habit of using it. They may not think much of its meaning; they may not understand its full import. No man and no angel does. But it is the true form of thought and affection, and it becomes the means of conjunction and communication between those who use it and the angels and the Lord. It is a vessel for the reception of spiritual life; it is an instrument of transmitting heavenly influences to the soul. It becomes "remains" in the secret chambers of the heart which may be vivified in some critical and favorable moment, and be the means of turning the balance of influence in favor of heaven. Even if no positive good is gained, some evil may be prevented. The habit of lifting up our thoughts to the Lord in any time of temptation, of joy or sorrow; when we are in doubt what course to pursue; when we feel our need of strength and guidance, will have a most important influence upon our progress in spiritual life.

2. We must ask by diligently seeking to secure the means of obtaining the bread which we need. We must procure and bring to the Lord the vessels which can receive and retain the bread we ask. The beggars who go from door to door provide a basket in which to receive what is given them. Divine truths are the only vessels which will receive and retain the bread of heaven. We must learn these truths from the Word. Spiritual truths are the only vessels which can receive and retain spiritual life. Natural truths will not. A man might know all the facts and principles and laws of the material world, if such an amount of knowledge were possible, without having a spiritual idea, or anything in his mind capable of receiving and being acted upon by the Holy Spirit which is

Divine truth. The memory must be stored and the understanding formed by Divine truths before the Lord can make us spiritual. He operates upon us by means of a force, an influence. There must be something in us to receive the force and be affected by it. The Lord cannot communicate a heavenly affection to a stone or to an animal, because there is nothing in them to receive it. The stone can be acted upon by heat and light; the animal can receive affection and sensation in low forms because it has an organization adapted to the forces which produce those effects. But sensation cannot be communicated to the stone, and a rational love to God and man cannot be given to the animal for the same reason. The ear does not ask for light, and light cannot be given to it, because it is not a vessel organized to receive it. The law is of universal application. We cannot think upon any subject or love any person of whom we have no knowledge.

If, therefore, we desire to receive the love of the Lord, which is the bread of life, we must learn truths which relate to Him. Divine truths are called in the Word spiritual riches. They are to man's spiritual progress and attainment as gold and silver and precious stones to supplying his natural wants and ministering to his natural delights. He should, therefore, be more eager and diligent in obtaining them in great abundance and variety than he is in acquiring natural wealth. He should seek for them as for hid treasure. He should pray for them morning, noon, and evening. He should store his memory with them. No two truths are exactly alike, consequently they do not receive precisely the same form of good. The bread will differ in quality; will be more or less adapted to sustain spiritual life; will differ in flavor and delicious power to nourish and enlarge our spiritual faculties as the truths which receive it differ in quality. As water takes on the form of the vessel which contains it, so the Divine love takes on the qualities of the truth which receives it. When we are learning Divine truths and storing our minds with them we are praying for our spiritual bread.

3. But a vessel will remain empty and render us no service unless we take it to the fountain and fill it. No asking is effective, and no prayer is complete until it becomes embodied in the deed. We may have an abundance of vessels and know where the bread is, but unless we put the bread into the basket; unless we eat it, it will not sustain and nurture our souls. We fill the truth with heavenly bread when we do what the truth tells us to do. When we begin to obey the commandments the love flows in. The Lord fills them with the bread of heaven; He gives us His flesh to eat. This is the most difficult part of the prayer; but it is the part which gives fulness and effect to the others. An illustration from natural bread will show this. We pray for material bread when we feel · the need of it, when we learn how to get it and actually procure it. But the hunger, which is the prayer of the body for bread, is not answered until we eat it and it becomes a part of its tissues. So the prayer of our spiritual bodies is not fully made and answered until we appropriate the love of the Lord, and it becomes a component part of our spiritual organism. The Divine love must be in us; it must be flowing through our spiritual arteries and conveying life to every organ, and become life as it is incorporated into it. This reception and appropriation of the Divine love takes place in the exercise of the affections which this love creates. We pray for this bread in every

act of keeping the commandments and in every effort to keep them. We pray this prayer when we shun evils as sins against God, and when we do good because it is from God and of God. We offer this petition when we perform any useful service to others from regard to their good.

Finally, let us consider more fully what is meant by " this day" and " daily" in its application to our spiritual sustenance and growth, for it is a most important part of the petition. Day, when translated into spiritual language, means state. It can have no reference to time or space, as there are no fixed times and spaces in the spiritual world, and these qualities of matter have no relation to the spirit. By daily is not meant simply enough bread for to-day, but support and nourishment for every possible state and degree of affection. The real meaning of this clause of the prayer is, Give me to-day what I need to-day. It is not a request that our Heavenly Father will give us to-day what we need for to-morrow and for all coming time, but what we need now. There is much more implied in this petition than appears upon the surface.

4. It implies entire trust in the Lord. It implies the conviction that He will do the best He can for us at all times and in all conditions. There is in the very nature of self-love a disposition to depend upon ourselves and to distrust the Lord. This is the cause of all our regrets for the past, all our corroding cares for the present, all our anxieties about the future. As we look back over the past and see how many of our plans have failed, how many mistakes we have made, how much suffering and sorrow have been caused by our ignorance, our wilfulness, our perversities, we sometimes feel

disposed to distrust the goodness and constant care of our Heavenly Father. Why did He not prevent us from taking some step which led to loss of health or property or friends, and to a long train of miseries? Why did He permit us to do a deed, to form some acquaintance, to make an alliance which has made life a failure and caused years of suffering and sorrow? There is a feeling that the Lord might have prevented these evils if He were disposed to do so. But He could not. He did the best He could for us at the time. He could not restrain us by principles which had no existence in our minds. He could not guide us by knowledge which we did not possess. He could not lead us by motives and affections which had never been awakened in our hearts. He cannot guide the ignorant by heavenly intelligence. He cannot lead the perverse and malignant will by heavenly affections. He restrained us from evil as fully as we would be restrained. Do we know how much He restrains us? How much sin, sorrow, and agony we should rush into if His restraining hand was not constantly laid upon us? We know nothing of what is prevented. What might have been if we had pursued a different course we can never tell. There are infinite paths leading from every point. Endless consequences result from every act. Every truth or falsity we learn, every good or evil affection we exercise, every deed we do modifies to some extent our eternal future. The Lord does the best He can every moment to restrain us from evil, to lead us in the wisest way, and to give us the bread we need.

We look upon great events as the controlling agencies of life, and as those which are specially under the direction of the Divine Providence. But this is not so. It is the little, daily constant acts and influences which cause the great events and become the controlling forces of life. The greater is made up of the less. The Lord acts in the leasts, and by means of them in the greatests. He feeds and sustains our spiritual life as He does our physical life momentarily, and in every least, infinitesimal point. He provides in the least parts for the whole and in every point of time for eternity. The whole of life is in every part. If we trust the Lord in the present we trust Him always. If we do our duty to-day according to our highest knowledge and ability we establish the strongest safeguards against evil and sorrow, and we make the surest provisions for our eternal good. To-morrow is the flower and fruitage of to-day; eternity, of time. " He that is faithful in that which is least is faithful also in much." The present is the only time in which we can act. The love and wisdom we possess is the only love and wisdom we can use. Let us then learn this prayer, " Give us this day our daily bread." Let us cease to mourn over the past; let us cease to fear or hope for the future; let us live in the present; let us do the work of the present; let us enjoy the good of the present; let us trust in the Lord for our bread to-day, and we shall trust Him forever; we shall not know any want; we shall be guided by the highest wisdom and we shall obtain the greatest good.

# X

# THE FORGIVENESS OF SIN.

---

*"And forgive us our debts, as we forgive our debtors.*

*" For if ye forgive men their trespasses, your Heavenly Father will also forgive you.*

*" But if ye forgive not men their trespasses, neither will your Heavenly Father forgive your trespasses."*—Matt. vi. 12, 14, 15.

In these words our Lord brings us face to face with the only obstacles which oppose our complete and eternal happiness. The Lord created all worlds, all living beings, and all material things to minister to human good ; and He gave to man capacities to receive good in some form and measure from everything He has made. He created man in a Divine order; made all his faculties both physical and spiritual, to harmonize with all substances and forces, so that they can act upon him and flow through him, become component parts of his own nature, call all his faculties into harmonious play, and by their own action enlarge their capacities and perfect their qualities for the reception of more exquisite happiness.

Sin has disturbed this order, changed these harmonies into discords, arrayed force against force, and brought man into conflict with nature and the Lord. It has induced weakness, paralysis of his spiritual faculties, disease, pain, misery, and death. Sin has inverted the whole order of his nature, and perverted the essential form and substance of his being. As man stood in the heavenly order of his creation he was endowed with a keen and delicate perception, a kind of spiritual instinct, by which he gained intuitive knowledge of the relations of all things to himself and the service they were created to render him. The hot breath of sin has withered and destroyed that faculty. In his normal condition man's heart was full of love to the Lord and man, and all his faculties were vivified, made fresh and sweet, and filled with a serene and joyful activity; sin has changed that love into enmity, poisoned the currents of that "river of life," and turned it into an instrument of torment and death. Man was made to be a help, a comfort, and a joy to man; sin has made him an Ishmaelite, a tyrant, and a curse. Every evil which human beings suffer is caused by sin; every good from the immeasurable fountain of life which man fails to obtain is withheld by sin. Sin opens the gates of hell, sin shuts the gates of heaven, sin is the only bar between man and the Lord.

Such being the hostile and deadly nature of sin, there is no question of so vital interest to every human being as how to escape its power and destroy this deadly enemy. Our Lord directs us to the only sufficient Helper, and He gives us the only conditions on which that help can be obtained, "Forgive us our debts, as we forgive our debtors." Let us try to understand what this prayer is; what desires, what knowledge, what action it implies; what we ask of the Lord, and what it demands of us.

Sin is called by different names to designate the different

points of view from which it is regarded. It is called a
debt because we are all the subjects of immutable law. We
are a part of the order of the universe, and only by acting
in obedience to the laws of this order can we obtain happiness. These laws have their origin in the Divine nature;
they are the order and methods according to which the
purposes of the Divine love and wisdom are carried into
effect. Man is folded in their arms; they are the paths of
the Lord, in which He comes to man and sends him life
and good. Man owes them obedience because he can only
gain the true end of his being by living according to them.
So far as he fails in obedience he becomes a debtor to the
law and the Lawgiver. He does not give what he owes to
them. This relation of debtor to the law is generally acknowledged, and is familiar to every one. We say a man owes
his success to his industry, to his talents, to his skill, or he
owes his failure to the want of these qualities or to some
mistakes he has made. Health is due to obedience to the
laws of man's physical nature. Disease and pain are due
to violations of those laws. Thus the idea of debt runs
through all human relations. But we must guard against
the fatal error of taking commercial indebtedness as the
measure and form of all debt. When we violate a law of
the Divine order embodied in our natures, or in human
society, we do not owe the *penalty* to the law or the lawgiver
in any other sense than we owe the good we receive to the
same cause when we obey a law. The penalty is not inflicted for violating it, nor is the reward conferred for obedience. Each follows as a necessary consequence. What
every human being really owes to the Lord, and consequently to all the laws of His order, is obedience. It is
not penalty or reward. We owe allegiance to the Lord

because that is the only way in which He can bestow upon us the blessings He created us to receive. When our Lord teaches us to ask Him to forgive our debts, then, He does not instruct us to ask for the remission of the penalties of sin, but for the remission of the sin itself.

Sin is also called a trespass. To trespass a rule or law is to go beyond it, to do what it does not allow. Transgression has the same meaning. But the word which our Lord used means stumbling. It does not seem to be so much a direct and positive determination to live contrary to the Divine laws, as ignorance of their nature and requirements, and a lack of spiritual power to walk erect and with a firm step, without any deviation or stumbling in the paths of the Lord. We are drawn aside by the illusions of the senses, we have never been taught what these laws are, we have become cramped by evil habits, we are weighted with many cares under whose burden we bend and fall. There are many obstacles in the way over which we stumble. How often those who are trying to live a good life stumble and fall, like little children who are learning to walk. How many are groping around in the dark! They stumble over unseen obstacles, they are led astray by others. We all have to learn to walk twice, first naturally, then spiritually, and the second lesson is by far the most difficult. But the difficulties consist wholly in our sins. They are the only stumbling-blocks. If man had never sinned it would have been as easy for him to live a heavenly life as it is for flowers to blossom and birds to sing. He would have been led on in the paths of the Divine truth, he would have been borne along in the currents of the Divine forces. All his faculties would have unfolded in a natural order by processes of delight. Sin is the only hindrance.

We must distinguish between sin and sinful acts. Sin is a disease of man's moral nature; it is derangement and perversion of the faculties of his spiritual organism, producing the same relative effects upon them that natural diseases cause in our physical organs. The real, essential prayer, then, must be that Our Father will restore us to spiritual health. The remission of the penalty is not the forgiveness of sin; it has no relation to it. The penalty of sin cannot be remitted while the sin remains, because it is inseparably connected with it. The penalty cannot be borne by another. That is as impossible as it would be for one man to be afflicted with disease and another to bear the pain and suffer the weakness. It is true that the sins of one man will bring suffering upon many others. It is true that we may undergo many hardships, endure severe labor and suffer pain of body and agony of mind in our efforts to relieve others from the penalties of their sins both physical and spiritual, but our sufferings do not help them. It is what we do for them, and not what we suffer. Society is organic. Individuals are members of the same body, and if one member is diseased, every member suffers; but the suffering does not cure the disease.

Our Lord suffered and died *for* us, but not in our stead. He took upon Himself our diseased and perverted nature. He went from village to village, from city to city, healing diseases, instructing the ignorant, and comforting the sorrowful. He wrestled in agony with man's spiritual enemies in Gethsemane, was crucified on Calvary, died, and rose again. It was necessary that He should assume our nature, for in no other way could He come into the material world, gain access to human beings, and bring His Divine and saving power to bear upon them. Only through this perverted organism could He come in conflict with the hosts of man's spiritual enemies and overcome them. The conflict and the agony were in the plane of the imperfect nature He assumed from Mary. That conflict was waged during His whole life upon the earth, and was attended with the most acute and awful agonies, agonies which forced the blood from His veins and wrung from Him the despairing cry, "My God, my God, why hast Thou forsaken me?" By these conflicts He glorified the nature He assumed, and made it the perfect medium of communicating His Divine power and life to men. The suffering did no more effect the work than the pain of a surgical operation contributes to its success. The suffering was caused by the work; it was itself an effect of it. Suffering has no saving efficacy; but the conflict with sin cannot be waged and the victory won, without exhausting labor and intense pain. The Lord's sufferings and death were not vicarious in the sense of being a substitute for the penalties which man brings upon himself by violating the laws of his nature.

What, then, is the forgiveness of sin? The answer to this question will depend upon what we understand by sin and its forgiveness. If we regarded sin simply in a commercial way, payment of the debt would be forgiveness, and this could be done by any one as well as by the debtor. If the penalty of sin is arbitrarily affixed by the lawgiver, like that which is attached to an act of the Legislature, it can be remitted by the same authority that enacted it, and on any conditions the legislator may determine. If a man commits murder and the law condemns him to death, the executive in whom is invested the pardoning power may remit the penalty. But the effect upon the man's character, the moral penalty, cannot be remitted by the mere good pleasure of man or the Lord. If one man assaults another, and in the conflict loses one of his eyes, he might be imprisoned, and afterwards pardoned; but no executive clemency or power could restore his eye. That is a penalty of the conflict which cannot be forgiven. A legal penalty may be forgiven, but those penalties which follow as the effects of violating an organic law of man's nature cannot be borne or remitted by others.

If we regard sin as a spiritual disease, as corruption in the will, blindness and disorder in the understanding, derangement and perversion of man's moral nature, then the forgiveness of sin consists in curing him of his spiritual diseases. It is the purification of his affections, it is the restoration of the understanding to its original order and normal condition, it is curing his spiritual blindness, giving him ears to hear the words of the Lord, and eyes to perceive the delicate and exquisite harmonies of the Divine order; it is putting all his faculties into right relations to each other and to the source of life. When this is done, and so far as it is done, the penalty also is remitted, for the penalty goes with the disease. When a musical instrument is out of tune the penalty is discord. Tune it and the penalty disappears. The Lord came into the world to restore our disorderly faculties to their normal condition, to bring them into harmony with the order of His own nature, to conjoin them to Him, as the branch to the vine, that the life-giving forces of His own nature might flow into them, cleanse them of their impurities, vivify them with His love, and cause them to bear fruit abundantly. When, therefore, we pray to the Lord to forgive us our debts, we must think of our own sinful natures, of our diseased and dying condition, and the burden and purpose of our prayer

11

must be that the Lord will heal our diseases, save us from the death they threaten, and conjoin us to Himself.

We must ask the Lord to forgive our sins, because He is the only Being who can do it. He is the Author of our nature, He organized its faculties and adjusted all their relations to one another, to the outward world, and to Himself. He only has the wisdom and power to restore them to their original soundness and order. He knows the only remedies that are efficacious, and the only conditions in which those remedies can be effectively applied. He is the only Physician who can cure us. We must go to Him in the spirit, with the same directness and urgency that we go to a physician when we are suffering from some severe bodily disease. When a man is filled with pain which has come upon him as the penalty for violating some law of his physical nature, he does not go to his physician as a mere formality, and ask him for help in the lifeless and meaningless way we too often utter the words of our text; he is in earnest. He knows what he wants. When the physician has heard his prayer, and tells him what to do and how to do it, he listens attentively, asks him to repeat the directions if he has any doubt about them, and then obeys them. We should go to the Lord in the same spirit, and be faithful in doing what He tells us to do. Let us take heed to the only conditions on which the Great Physician declares we can be forgiven. He does not ask us to pray for unconditional forgiveness. "Forgive us our debts, as we forgive our debtors." He does not teach us to say, "Forgive us our debts," because the Saviour has cancelled them. He does not teach us to say, "Forgive us our debts," because the Lord Jesus Christ has suffered and died for us. There is no intimation of any vicarious work having been performed, no appeal for mercy on the ground of the merits of another person. The only conditions are that we forgive others :

"*For if ye forgive men their trespasses, your Heavenly Father will also forgive you; But if ye forgive not men their trespasses, neither will your Heavenly Father forgive your trespasses.*"

From this declaration, which is presented in an affirmative and a negative form to make it as clear and strong as possible, we are taught that the Lord will only forgive us as we forgive others. It is of essential importance, therefore, that we understand what is meant by the forgiveness of others. Our salvation depends upon it. We cannot suppose that nothing more than the common idea of forgiveness is implied in these conditions; that the Lord will not punish us for our offences against Him if we do not punish others for their offences against us. There must be some law of the Divine wisdom involved in this condition, some reasons founded in the essential relations between the Lord and man. Let us try to discover what they are. It will help us to come to just conclusions if we keep in mind what forgiveness essentially is not. It is not the remission of the penalty. The Lord does not say to men, If you will not punish others, I will not punish you. The forgiveness of sin has no direct reference to its penalty. The penalty is the effect, the mere shadow of the sin. It does not consist in cherishing a feeling of complacency and friendship for those who have injured us; we cannot do that. We are, indeed, commanded "to love our enemies, to bless them that curse us, do good to them that hate us, and pray for them which despitefully use us and persecute us." But we may love our enemies without feeling a personal affection for them. We really love others when we desire to restrain them from evil and help them to overcome it. The form our love takes will depend upon the condition of others. We may seek their punishment from the kindest regard to them. To forgive others consists "in regarding them from a principle of good," that is, from a sincere desire to do them good, and, so far as lies in our power, in doing them good as we have opportunity.

We must forgive their trespasses. By trespasses, as we have seen, are meant stumblings in the way of life, falling into error, wandering from the true path, failure in duty. To forgive others when they stumble consists in removing the cause of stumbling, whether that cause is in ourselves, as is often the case, or in them. This is the essential part of the work, and it should begin with ourselves. We sincerely and effectively offer this petition when we so regulate our actions by the commandments that they will not be the cause of offence or stumbling to those with whom we associate. By our conduct we exercise a much greater power over others to help or hinder them in the way to heaven than we do by our words. A good life is the best sermon; it is a constant influence which tends to restrain, to guide, to cheer; it is generally regarded as the best evidence and test of the truth of the doctrines professed. On the other hand, men and women who do not live up to their profession, or are not in the constant efforts to do so, are a stumbling-block to every one within the circle of their influence. They cause the value of truth to be depreciated, they awaken doubts with regard to the value of a religious life, they cause the simple to err, the irresolute to falter, the weak to fall. Every one who lives a pure, truthful, upright, and useful life is forgiving the trespasses of others, is offering this petition in a sincere and effective manner, and is complying with the only conditions on which his own trespasses can be forgiven.

But we must not only set good examples, we must do all in our power to communicate the truth to others. Genuine truth is the path which leads to heaven. It is a luminous path shining with its own light. Ignorance is darkness, error is a false way, and those who follow it wander in darkness. Trespasses are specifically sins against the truth, they are false principles. The only effective way to forgive men their trespasses is to lead them into the truth. Parents offer this prayer for their children when they instruct them in the doctrines of the church. Every faithful Sunday-school teacher is laboring to forgive the trespasses of the children he teaches. Whenever we converse with others for the purpose of correcting an error by giving the truth, every book we lend, every tract we distribute for the purpose of making known the truth, we are trying to forgive the trespasses of others.

But everything we do or say will be far more efficient in forgiving others when we act from love to them. Love gives warmth, power, life to what we say and do. It gives wings to our words, it endows our example with a winning and attractive power, it disposes the mind to listen to our words, to read attentively what we offer, it gains the listening ear, and tends to soften and open the affections to receive what we have to give. The ways in which we can forgive others are innumerable, and some of these ways are within the reach of every one. As we use the means we have, we are complying with the conditions on which the Lord will forgive our trespasses.

Such being the clear and emphatic teachings of the Lord

in His Word, every thoughtful and rational mind must desire to know why the Lord makes these conditions? Does He base His action upon ours? Does He make our love for others the measure of His love for us, our action towards others the guide of His action towards us? He is love; we are only the contracted and perverted forms of receiving it. Our love to His is not so much as the drop to the ocean. His wisdom is infinite; our light compared with His is not so much as the faintest ray to the unclouded sun. He possesses infinite power; we are weak and frail, the most helpless of created beings. Why, then, should He condition His action on ours, and measure what He will do for us by what we do for others? A satisfactory answer to this question can only be found in a true knowledge of what we are and of our relations to the Lord and to men.

We are only recipients of life. All our faculties are organic vessels for the reception and transmission of life in the forms of power, wisdom, and love. No vessel can receive more than it can contain. No organ can receive a different quality of life than that which it was formed to receive. The eye cannot hear, the tongue cannot see, the heart cannot admit the atmosphere. The Lord cannot give us any more than we can receive. As He cannot give us any more light than the eye can admit, so He cannot give us any more truth than the understanding can receive. The limit of every material organ to bear the influx of heat is soon reached. If we pass beyond it, the organization is destroyed. So, if the Lord should pour His Divine love, which is substance and power in their very essence, with full intensity into our affections, we should be consumed in a moment. He cannot give us any more love than we can receive. He cannot give it to us in any higher and purer forms than we can receive it. He is, therefore, limited both in the quality and quantity of His gifts or of what He can do for us, by'our capacities of reception. Omnipotence cannot give us what we cannot take.

We are not merely passive recipients of life; if we were, the Lord would fill every vessel full to the extent of its capacity. We are voluntary recipients; we can close our hearts against the currents of the Divine love; we can shut our understandings against the truth, as we can close our eyes against the light. The Lord has endowed us with this power. He has made us free agents. Moral freedom is essential to our humanity. The Lord always respects it. He teaches us the truth, and He tries to lead us to a heavenly life by all the influences He can bring to bear upon us; but He always leaves us in freedom to act of ourselves, for only what we do in freedom is our own act. If we will not live according to the commandments which are laws of life, He cannot compel us. Here again we can see that there is a limit to what the Lord can do for us. He can only give us what we are willing to receive. Let us consider another point and then we may be able to see why the Lord will not, or cannot, which is the same, forgive us our trespasses unless we forgive others. It is evident that, if man receives all his life from the Lord as a constant gift, his faculties must be adjusted to the influent forces of life with the most exquisite precision. Any deviation from their true order would interrupt or derange the currents of these forces and disturb their normal effects. It would destroy their qualities; it would change good to evil, truth to falsity, light to darkness, harmony to discord; it would invert the order of man's life, bring him into hostile relations to the Lord. This must be so in the

nature of things.  Man's spiritual faculties are adjusted to
spiritual forces, in the same way that his material faculties
are adjusted to material forces.  Any derangement or
deviation from the order of its forms fills the eye with
pain, and if the trespass continues entirely incapacitates it
to receive the light.  The same law applies to every organ
in the body.  How can the eye be forgiven its trespasses?
Evidently by restoring it to its normal condition and true
relations to the light.  There is no other way.  The same
wise and inexorable law of the Divine order applies to the
mind, which is a spiritual organism.  If its forms are
deranged by misuse, its trespass can only be forgiven by
restoring them to their true order and tone.  The two
fundamental laws of spiritual life are love to the Lord and
man.  This is the true order of his life.  Our faculties were
made by infinite wisdom to act in that way.  And our
Lord declares this in the most explicit manner:

"*Jesus said, The first of all the commandments is, Hear,
O Israel, the Lord our God is one Lord: And thou shalt
love the Lord thy God with all thy heart, and with all thy
soul, and with all thy mind, and with all thy strength.*

"*And the second is like unto it, Thou shalt love thy
neighbor as thyself.  On these two commandments hang
all the Law and the Prophets.*"

When a man loves himself supremely he sins, he
stumbles and falls away from true order; he trespasses
against the Lord and his neighbor; he inverts the whole
order of his nature, makes that the supreme end of life
which was intended, in the constitution of his faculties, to
be secondary and instrumental.  His affections become
corrupted, his understanding darkened.  Disorder, confusion, and anarchy are introduced into the mind.  The

ideas are distorted, and all the criterions of right are
destroyed. We become subject to illusions, we wander
from the true path, we stumble and fall. This disorderly
and evil condition can only be changed by a change in the
organization of the mind. These trespasses against
perfections of the Divine order embodied in man's nature
can only be forgiven by replacing the diseased faculties
with new, sound, and orderly ones. We must be born from
above, we must be regenerated and made anew.

But this can only be done by our co-operation. We are
not in the Lord's hands like a block of marble in the
sculptor's. Our freedom must be respected; we must be
led by sufficient motives "to cease to do evil," and we
must learn to do well. This is the process and condition
in all changes in our characters. We must learn the truth,
and then we must cease to think and do what it forbids,
and we must understand and do what it commands. In
this way the old, perverted, corrupt forms of the mind are
removed, and new faculties, fashioned according to the laws
of the Divine order, take their place. As this work of
transformation goes on our iniquities are blotted out, our
debts, trespasses, transgressions are forgiven, our sins are
remitted. This work of healing and restoration is effected
by the Lord, by the forces of life which constantly flow
from Him, as light and heat from the sun. But it can
only be effected while man co-operates with Him. He
cannot forgive our sins while we continue sinning; He cannot fill our hearts with love to Him and the neighbor
while we continue to love ourselves and the world supremely. It is evident that He can only forgive—that is,
give up and put away—our sins as we turn to Him and try
to put ourselves in right relations to Him.

Now we may be able to see why the Lord can only forgive us as we forgive others. When we begin to regard others from love and a sincere desire to help them to overcome their evils, to teach them the truth, to lead them back into the path of life, to remove so far as lies in our power all causes of stumbling, to lift them up when they fall, to strengthen them in their weakness, to encourage them when they despair; when we feel kindly towards others, whatever may be their character and condition, and stand ready to help them according to their needs and our ability; in a word, when it is the purpose and effort of our lives to forgive the trespasses of others, we are coming into true relations to them and the Lord. The currents of the Divine love, which, like the blood in the body, contain all cleansing, healing, invigorating, and perfecting substances and forces, begin to flow through us, and forgive our trespasses. They organize a new will, create a new understanding, and restore to us the lost likeness and image of our Heavenly Father. This is the way in which the Lord forgives us our debts, as we forgive our debtors. We offer this prayer when, and only when, we forgive the debts of others, and the Lord forgives us our trespasses as much and as little as we forgive others. Our forgiveness of others is the measure of His forgiveness of us.

# XI

# TEMPTATION.

---

*"And lead us not into temptation."*—Matt. vi. 13.

THE instruction which our Lord gives us in these words is of supreme importance; it touches our vital and eternal interests. In some form and in some degree every one is tempted, and no one can be regenerated without passing through its fires, enduring its torments, resisting its allurements, and subduing the enemies who cause it. It is a subject about which little has been known or can be known without some true knowledge of the sources of our life, the spiritual forces which are continually operating upon us, and the spiritual beings who are intimately associated with us on the spiritual side of our nature, and who, consequently, touch the secret springs of thought and affection, and exercise a controlling influence in the formation of a wicked or a heavenly character.

The New Church has truths to teach upon this subject which throw much light upon it. They place us in a central point of view above the illusion of appearances, where

171

we can see effects in their causes; where we can learn the origin and understand the nature of temptations, and see the foes who assault us. They put weapons into our hands which the tempters cannot resist, teach us how to wield them, and where to find wisdom to foil their most cunning strategy, and strength to resist their most powerful attacks. I ask your devout and earnest attention to what our doctrines teach upon this subject. We cannot offer this petition with our hearts and understandings without a clear and true knowledge of what temptation is. The first point for our consideration must, therefore, be, What is temptation?

The doctrines of the New Church give a clear and specific answer to this question, an answer founded in the nature of the human mind, of man's relations to the spiritual beings with whom he is associated, and the teachings of the Lord in the Sacred Scriptures. Temptations are the conflicts of the internal man with the external, or of the spiritual man with the natural. Some knowledge of the organization of the human mind is essential to a clear understanding of this definition. The human mind is composed of three planes or degrees entirely distinct from each other, as distinct as the bones, flesh, and nerves in the material body. They were made to act together as one, as all the degrees of organic forms in the material body act together as one. But still they are so distinct that they can act separately; they can even act in opposition to one another. Each degree is so full and variously organized that it is a man in itself, and is capable of performing all the functions of a man. It has a will and understanding, affections, desires, thoughts, and acts appropriate to that degree of life. These degrees or planes are called the natural, the spiritual, and the celestial man respectively. The natural man is not the material body which constitutes no essential part of our nature, but the lowest degree of the human mind. The complete man is, therefore, a threefold or trinal being.

These three degrees of the mind exist in potency in every human being; but the natural degree is first in the order of creation. This is necessarily so, because it forms the basis for the higher degrees of the mind, and through its instrumentality the means are provided for their creation, as the material body is the instrument by which the natural man lives in this world and can use material things for the formation of natural ideas and affections. The natural man was intended to be the servant of the spiritual man, and the spiritual man of the celestial, and in a true order of life these three planes of the human mind act in perfect harmony with each other, and all with the Lord. But the natural man has become wholly evil. The organic forms of his nature have become wholly deranged and inverted. This degree of man's nature he derives from his parents, and it is full of hereditary evils. This is the part of man's nature which has fallen. The spiritual and celestial degrees have never become false and evil; they have never lost their purity and heavenly perfection, because they remain as a mere possibility in every one so long as he continues in sin, like the germ of a seed which never grows. This is the new man who is born from above. This degree of man's nature is organized according to all the substances and forces and order of heaven, as the natural man and the material body are organized with relation to the substances and forces and order of the material world. They are entirely distinct in their capacities, they dwell in distinct worlds. They are as distinct as the eye and the ear. The eye dwells in the world of light, the ear in the atmospheric world, and neither of them can perform any of the other's functions, or know anything of the other's joys.

As the natural plane of the mind, which, as I have said, was created to be the servant of the spiritual mind and to act in subordination to it, has become evil and false, full of the love of self and of the world, and seeks its own gratification in all its desires and activities, it is hostile to the spiritual mind. It is directly opposed to it in all its ends, methods, and desires. The natural man hates what the spiritual man loves. All their principles, ideas, and activities are diametrically opposite. Consequently, as soon as the spiritual man begins to manifest any life, and to take possession of the natural man and use him as his servant, bring him into obedience, and direct his affections, thoughts, and actions, there arises a combat, and this combat is temptation. It is a conflict between evil spirits and angels for the possession of man's soul. Man's own nature is the battle-field, and the weapons the combatants wield are the evils and falsities, on the one hand, and the good affections and truths on the other, which they can find in his own mind.

All our life comes from a spiritual origin. We are so intimately connected with spirits and angels that all power of thought and affection is due to their influence. Man has no more self-derived power to will, think, and act than a statue of marble. If his connection with the spiritual world and its inhabitants was entirely severed, he would have no more power to perform any mental or natural act than the material body has when the spirit has left it. This combat is waged, therefore, by the spiritual beings who are in the most intimate connection with him, who touch by their influence the most secret springs of his nature. It

is not a conflict of words, an argument for and against certain dogmas or courses of action, but of influence over
man. The evil spirits act upon his lusts and false principles; endeavor to excite them into activity and lead man
to act wickedly. They breathe into his love of self and
try to kindle it into a consuming flame. They flow into his
love of the world and awaken an intense desire for wealth
and power. They excite his natural passions and appetites,
and stimulate his ambition, his vanity and pride, and by the
most cunning arts blind him to the truth; make the false
appear as the true, and the true as the false. They labor
to fix his attention upon some natural or sensual delight,
and then they magnify it and glorify it to make it appear
to be essential to happiness. They offer a present delight,
and hold it so closely before the mind's eye that it conceals
the inevitable and terrible consequences. They solicit with
almost superhuman skill, and weave enchantments around
the soul with surpassing cunning. They quiet fears, they
kindle hopes, they promise the kingdoms of this world
with their power and glory, they offer bread for stones, and
protection from every harm. They are constantly present,
and unremitting in their efforts to destroy us body and
soul, under the guise of ministering to our happiness and
making us as gods. It is not great crimes alone which are
due to their influence. They awaken pride, they foster
vanities, they inflame hatreds, they excite revenges, they
taint the innocent souls of boys and girls with impurities,
and urge them along in the currents of their natural desires. Could young men and women see them as they are
in all their horrid deformities; could they know that the
power which excites their love of self and the world was the
hot and rank breath of infernal beings who, under the guise

of friends leading them to happiness, are poisoning their souls and planting in their affections the seeds of ruin, sorrow, and despair; could they see this they would stop their ears against their siren voices, they would cry out to them, "Get thee behind me, Satan;" they would flee from them as they would flee from pestilence and eternal death.

The angels, on the other hand, seek to awaken every good affection, and to place before the attention every genuine truth. Some act directly upon the affections, the secret springs of life. They seek to bring into consciousness the innocent affections implanted in the mind in infancy and childhood. Many a young man and woman has been saved from spiritual death by the memory of a mother's love and unselfish devotion. In some critical moment, when the decision hung in even balance, the scale has been turned in favor of heaven and eternal life by the recollection of some tender ministry of a mother's quenchless love, or some truth gained from a father's instruction. Do you suppose that influence came of itself? Did that recollection leap from the memory where it had been buried for years under the dust and decaying forms of false principles and evil deeds? No. Some angel came in the guise of the mother's patient loveliness, and spoke in the tones of her remembered voice, brought into vivid light some Divine truth learned from the Bible or taught in the Sunday-school, or lisped at the mother's knee, called into activity all the innocent affections associated with it, and the tempter was foiled and the soul was saved.

It is the office of other angels whose genius fits them for the special service, to act upon the intellectual faculties. With bright and keen intelligence they run through the mind and discover every idea of truth existing there, and by heavenly skill bring it out from the dark recesses of the memory, and place it in bright and clear distinctness before the attention that it may gain recognition, and that the mind, darkened by error, may see as in a mirror some glimpses of the order and beauty and substantial good of heaven. They are diligent and faithful in their office, for they delight in it. They love us with an unselfish and an unchanging love, and it is the joy of their hearts to render us any service.

Their influence and service does not, however, come to the attention with the distinctness and gross power of the evil spirits, because they operate upon the more interior and unconscious parts of our nature; but their influence is none the less powerful. The reluctance which is at first generally felt against the commission of sin, the drawing back of the thoughts and the affections as by some attraction, the fears which are excited, the shame which follows detection, the resolutions to shun the evil, and the manifold influences which operate upon the mind to awaken and develop heavenly affections, to fill the understanding with the light of heavenly truths, as the sun quickens to life every seed by its warmth and reveals the beauty of material objects by its light, is due to the influence of the angels. When we are striving to suppress the love of self and the world, when we feel ashamed of our vanities, our unkindness, our indifference to the wants and unhappiness of others; when we feel kindly towards others, and seek to render them a service, when we try to elevate our thoughts and affections to the Lord, and desires are awakened to do His will, we may know that the angels are present with us with as much certainty as though we could see their faces glowing with heavenly love, and hear their voices sweet and winning, with heavenly melodies.

12

O, my friends, we are girt about by awful mysteries. Every human being is beleaguered by hosts of spiritual beings who are contending for his possession. The evil spirits would blast every hope and destroy every capacity for heaven, drag us down to hell, and make miserable slaves of us forever. The angels seek to develop every germ of goodness, and unfold every faculty in the order and beauty of heaven. They seek to restore the lost image and likeness of our Heavenly Father, and make us His children and heirs of His infinite wealth of goodness and truth.

Such being our position, the questions naturally arise: Are we then the passive objects of these contending hosts? Are we simply a neutral territory with no agency in the conflict? By no means. We decide the battle. Neither devil nor angel can take possession of us without our consent. The Lord constantly gives us this power. When evil spirits inflame the lusts and passions of the natural mind and incite us to evil, we can refuse to follow their counsels. We can refuse to cherish the evil affections, to indulge in the impure and false thoughts, and especially to do the wicked deeds they incite us to commit. When we resist these enemies they leave us for a season until they can find some new avenue of approach. As they recede the angels draw nearer and take a firmer and more secure possession of our natures, and imbue them with the love and wisdom, the purity and harmony of a heavenly life. If, on the other hand, we consent to the wiles and allurements of our spiritual enemies, they grasp us with a more relentless power, they darken our understandings and weave around our affections a web of influences which seem soft as silk at first, but which in the end harden into fetters of iron. They benumb our spiritual faculties and close their doors against influx from the angels, and through them from the Lord. Every time we resist the efforts of our spiritual enemies to gain possession of our affections which constitute the citadel of life, we weaken the force of their hold upon us; every time we yield to their solicitations we come more fully into their power. We stand between these two contending hosts as Moses stood upon the hill during the battle between Israel and Amalek. When we hold up our hand, that is when we use the power the Lord has given us, and lift up the standard of Divine truth, our enemies are discomfited; when we let down our hand, Amalek, which is only another name for our most subtle enemies, wins the victory. Our hands often grow weary in this conflict, and we should utterly fail if we were not supported by the Divine truth, represented by the stone upon which Moses sat, and "Aaron and Hur who stayed up his hands, the one on the one side and the other on the other side."

Such, in general, is the nature of temptation. It is not merely allurement to evil; that is only one side of it. It is not merely a conflict between the abstract qualities of good and evil, truth and falsity. There is no power in external objects, in themselves, to excite the lusts of selfish and worldly affections; they are only the instruments which intelligent beings use to accomplish their purposes of good or evil. Abstract qualities have no existence separate and distinct from their subjects. Good and evil, truth and falsity, have no existence except in personal and intelligent beings. I present this subject, therefore, as it is, as a conflict between human beings for the possession of a distinct object. The conflict of two nations for a boundary-line, or a piece of territory, or dominion over the other, is not

more personal, distinct, and real than the hostile hosts who
are contending for the dominion of every human soul. It
is a real conflict waged by substantial human beings on the
spiritual plane of life, with art and skill and strategy, and
weapons of keener edge than Damascus blades, and it is a
conflict that is waged to decisive victory. It is a conflict
for dominion over a larger and more precious kingdom than
the whole world. Yes, my friends, we are the objects
aimed at in this war. One party desires to make every one
of us, our sons and daughters, miserable slaves and consign
us to hopeless bondage. The other, to free us from every
burden, and hindrance, and sorrow, and bring us into perfect
freedom, and endow us with the beauty, the order, the riches,
the joy of heaven, and the companionship of the angels.

Temptation is of various degrees; its special quality is
determined by the plane of the mind on which the battle
is fought. There can be no real temptation until the distinctly spiritual degree of the mind begins to come into
actual existence. Natural allurements are not properly
temptations. "Misfortunes, sorrows, and anxieties which
arise from natural and corporeal causes and bodily pains
and diseases" are not temptations, though they serve in
some degree to subdue and break the life of man's pleasures
and cupidities, and determine and elevate his thoughts to
interior and pious subjects. But there is no internal conflict between good and evil, truth and falsity, for there are
no grounds for it. If there is any conflict it is between
the natural gratification and natural fears of punishment,
or loss of reputation, or favor, or some natural good.

Spiritual temptation takes place in the understanding,
and is a conflict between truth and falsity, or between those
evil spirits who act specifically upon man's intellectual

faculties, and the angels in the corresponding plane of the mind. The evil spirits bring forth all man's falsities, and erroneous opinions and dogmas, and endeavor to persuade him that they are truths. They change truths into falses, and by the most alert and cunning legerdemain defend error, and make the true appear to be false and the false to be true. Herein lies the great difficulty in gaining a reception for a new truth. It cannot be done until the old error is removed. But our opinions and doctrines are intrenched in habits of thought, and entwined with associations from which it is difficult to break away. This temptation is often very severe, and the conflict continues for many years. Many of you, doubtless, have passed through this warfare and know by experience what it is. You were educated in a different faith from the one you now accept, and the transition has been more or less painful. First arose doubts about the truth of the old faith. It did not seem rational; it did not answer your questions, or satisfy the wants of your heart. So you doubted and feared, clung to the old faith and tried to make it appear to be true; turned here and there; fled for refuge to some new phase of thought, to find it untenable, and it may be, after many fruitless efforts, settled down in a state of despair of ever finding the light. But it came, as it always will come to every earnest and sincere seeker for it. All these varied experiences did not spring up spontaneously in the mind. They were the effects of spiritual conflicts between the angels of truth and error for the possession of the understanding.

The third and most severe temptation takes place in the will and the affections. The evil spirits excite man's appetites, desires, and carnal lusts; they inflame and intensify the love of self and the world, and so involve his whole consciousness in them that he cannot see any other good than their gratification. On the other hand, the angels defend and protect him by calling into activity the good and innocent affections that were awakened in infancy and childhood, and the truths which had been stored up in the memory. They turn the light of these truths directly upon the evil and false principles excited by wicked spirits, and in every possible way seek to disclose their impurities, deformities, and the terrible consequences which must result from their indulgence. This temptation is often attended with the most exquisite suffering, for it touches the most sensitive part of our nature. It is described in the Word by the most intense physical pain and the surrender of the most precious possessions. It is selling all we have and giving to the poor; it is leaving father, mother, houses, and lands, and following the Lord. It is cutting off the right hand, plucking out the right eye, taking up the cross, and laying down the life. With every regenerate soul it continues until he comes into states of despair, and the prayer is wrung from the tortured spirit, "If it be possible, let this cup pass from me," or the more despairing cry, "My God, my God, why hast thou forsaken me?"

Such being the nature of temptations, it is evident that no one can be regenerated without undergoing them. The distinctly spiritual plane of our being can be brought into substantial existence and conscious activity only as the loves of self and the world are subdued, and the natural mind, with its thoughts, affections, and cupidities, submits to be guided by the spiritual and heavenly. This conquest can only be effected "little by little," as the native inhabitants who represent our evils and falsities were driven out of the land of Canaan, and after many severe and terrible conflicts. Temptations, which are not merely allurements to sin, but actual conflicts with those who inflame our evil passions, are an essential means of regeneration. By temptations the diseased, inflamed, and perverted forms of the natural or external man are separated from the internal man, as the hard and coarse shell of a nut is separated from the internal and essential part of it by the power of frost. Temptations tend to give the good in us dominion over the evil, and the true over the false. They give us a clearer apprehension of truths, and lead us to practice them, while at the same time they subdue our evil affections and disperse the false principles derived from them. The spiritual man gains strength by the conflict. The organic vessels which compose the spiritual degree of the mind are developed and opened for the reception of larger currents of power from the angels and the Lord. The hardness and obduracy of the natural mind is softened in the fires of the conflict, and the loves of self and the world are subdued. The evil desires and cupidities become quiescent, and when the conquest is fully completed the heavenly man reigns supreme in the plane of natural life. Love to the Lord and man become the dominating motives in all natural pursuits; the Lord's will begins to be done on the earth of the natural mind as it is in the heaven of the spiritual mind.

But while it is true that we cannot be regenerated without temptations, the Lord never tempts us or leads us into them. He is in the constant effort to lead us out of them, and to deliver us from evil. He never assaults the wicked, nor do the angels who are His agents and ministers in leading men to heaven. They protect and defend man from the assaults of his enemies; but they never commence the attack. When evil spirits assault us and try to rob us of our priceless treasures, those who defend us do not lead into the conflict and are not responsible for it. Our Lord was led by the Spirit into the wilderness to be tempted, but the temptation was caused by the devil. Every action must be judged by the motives of the actor.

But it may be asked, "If the Lord never leads us into temptation, why did He teach us to ask Him not to do that which He never does?" This is a question which there have been many unsatisfactory attempts to answer. The answer doubtless is that this is spoken according to the appearance to us from a natural point of view, and is of the same character as a multitude of other passages in the Word in which qualities of character and changes are attributed to the Lord which take place in men. The fiercest passions which rage in the human heart are attributed to the Lord. He is represented as jealous, angry, revengeful, furious, as hating, tormenting, sending famine, pestilence, and war, and punishing with eternal death. He is also said to perform human and finite actions. He comes and goes, hides and manifests Himself; sends messengers to inquire as though He were ignorant, resolves and repents, and performs many other actions which would be wholly inconsistent with an omnipresent, omniscient, and infinitely wise Being. In all these cases the Lord is represented as He appears to man, and not as He is in Himself. The changes and actions which take place in us are attributed to the Lord, because it so seems to us. The Scriptures are written from a human as well as a Divine point of view. If they had not been, man could not have understood them in any sense, and they would not have been a revelation to him. The genuine truth is that the Lord does not lead man into temptation. He is in the constant effort to lead us into the peace and rest of heaven. But this cannot be done without temptation. The obstacles which lie in the way must be removed, the enemies must be overcome. From a natural point of view the trial, the conflict, the self-denial are all we can see. He says we must forsake father, and mother, and earthly possessions, and take up our cross and lay down our life. It seems to the natural mind that He is leading us into these privations and trials, and we can see no light, no peace, no good beyond them. They are the limits of our vision. It is natural that we should shrink from the sacrifice and conflict. Our Lord Himself did, and prayed that if possible He might be spared from drinking the bitter cup. The Lord has accommodated His Word to our limited apprehension. But in other places He has revealed the genuine truth, by which we can correct the natural appearance, as science corrects the illusions of the senses.

From our point of view, and according to our limited vision, the form of the petition is the true one; it is adapted to our state, it is the form which the Divine love and mercy must take in coming down to our apprehension; it is the negative side of the positive truth, expressed in the next clause, "but deliver us from evil." That is what the Lord is in the constant effort to do. He does not lead us into temptation, but He leads us while we are in it, He protects and supports us while we are undergoing it, and though He seems to have forsaken us and left us to struggle alone, yet He is really nearer to us than at any other time. He sympathizes with us, for "He was tempted in all points as we are." He has passed through every possible form of temptation, He has been where we are, and He knows how to succor and lead us. We cannot be delivered from evil until we overcome the enemies who cause it. The Lord is on our side in this conflict, and He is fighting against our enemies. We cannot find peace until the evils which disturb our repose are removed. The Lord is constantly saying to us, " My peace I leave with you, my peace I give unto you," and He employs every possible agency to bestow it upon us in the fullest and richest form.

How, then, shall we offer this prayer? By avoiding every allurement which leads to evil, by rejecting from our thoughts every suggestion of evil. When such thoughts arise in our minds we must attribute them to the presence of some evil spirit. Our thoughts are the words of the spiritual beings who are present within, and we must give them a prompt and indignant rejection. We must arm ourselves with weapons from the Word, and use them as our Lord did. A " thou shalt not" from the Lord is a sufficient reason for rejecting every evil suggestion. We must ask the Lord to deliver us from the evils or wicked beings who tempt us. In the degree we do this, we shall pray to our Father in secret, and He will reward us openly.

# XII

## DELIVERANCE FROM EVIL. WHAT IT IS, AND HOW EFFECTED.

---

"*And lead us not into temptation, but deliver us from evil.*"—Matthew vi. 13.

IT was the purpose of the discourse upon the first clause of this petition to show what temptations are, what causes them, and what purpose they serve in our regeneration. We found them to be combats between the internal and the external man, or between evil spirits and angels who operate upon these planes of man's nature for the possession of his soul. They are caused by their efforts to take possession of our wills and intellectual faculties, and bind us to them and to the societies with which they are associated by those spiritual ties which are stronger than any natural or material bonds. Temptation is not a conflict of words, or arguments, or personal strength, but of power over those who are tempted. The evil spirits act upon our worldly and selfish affections; they excite our appetites and inflame our passions; they seek to immerse our whole nature in vile

187

and corrupting influences. The angels, on the other hand, act upon all that is innocent, true, and good in us. They call up truths from the memory and present them bright and clear to our awakened attention; they breathe warmth and life into our languid spiritual affections, and by the attractions of their love they lift us up and draw us toward heaven and the Lord.

These opposing forces take effect upon us and draw us in two opposite directions; they come to our consciousness as distinctly as do opposing forces acting upon the body, and seem to us to spring up spontaneously within us and to be our own in their causes as well as in their effects. They are felt as doubts and fears, as anxieties and pains of conscience and stings of remorse. When these opposing forces which are struggling for dominion are powerful, and the theatre of the conflict is the more interior and sensitive planes of our nature, the pain is intense; we become distracted, literally drawn asunder; we are in agony, and fall into despair. Such was the experience of our Lord in Gethsemane and upon Calvary. This conflict and all the pain of it is caused wholly by evil, or by the evil spirits who seek to gain possession of our souls. They are the cause of all our pain, suffering, and sorrow of every kind. There is no abstract evil; there are no abstract causes. Evil is not a vague, indefinite, and unsubstantial entity. It has its origin in personal beings; it has no existence separate from them. There can be no murder without a murderer; there can be no theft without a thief; there can be no drunkenness without drunkards; there can be no envy, malice, pride, hatred, cruelty, or vice of any kind without human beings who exercise these evils. So there can be no temptation without personal and intelligent beings who tempt. Whenever we feel the movements of any desire to think falsely, or to act wickedly, if we attributed it to the influence of some evil being who was near us, inciting us to sin, we should regard the temptation in a very different manner from what we do when we think of it as a spontaneous action of the soul. If a man or woman met us on the street and openly solicited us to do what sometimes comes to us in inclination and thought, we should shrink with horror from the tempter. But the inclination and thought is as surely due to personal influence by personal beings, by men or women who have put off the garment of the material body and can now approach us directly on the spiritual side of our nature, as the temptations which come from human beings in a material body. They are all due to evil spirits, though in one case they are clothed in a material body, and in the other they are not.

With this idea of the personal nature of sin we can see the force of the petition, " Deliver us from evil." We do not look off into vacuity for some vague and incomprehensible help for deliverance from some abstract enemy. We go to a personal Being and implore help to rescue us from the power of personal enemies. There is something tangible, substantial, and definite for the thought to rest upon. If your little son or daughter had been stolen from you and carried into some den of infamy and cruelty, where it would become polluted and destroyed body and soul, your prayer for that child would not be a mere formality for its deliverance from some vague and imaginary danger. You would not be content to offer a petition in a cold and formal manner to some abstract power called the state, or the police. You would go to persons who are the embodiment of the power you invoke. Our sons and daughters are beset by spiritual enemies who are seeking to decoy them from their Father's house, to rob them of their inheritance of heavenly possessions, and make them the miserable slaves of sin. If we believed this, should we not pray in a more direct and effective manner for their deliverance from the power of these enemies?

Every human being must desire to be delivered from evil, but there is the widest diversity of opinions concerning what evil is. Every one judges from his own point of view, and that point of view is his dominant love, or principle of action. Everything which opposes this love, or the essential end for which he lives, he regards as evil, and every being who stands in the way of the attainment of that end he regards as an enemy. We cannot, therefore, make any human standard the absolute criterion of good or evil; we must have a universal and immutable and perfect rule. Such a standard can only be found in the Lord, who is "the way, the truth, and the life," and who "is the same yesterday, to-day, and forever." "I am the Lord; I change not." Let us then regard the subject, as far as possible, from a Divine point of view as revealed in the Sacred Scriptures, and in the doctrines of the New Church which are derived from them. So far as we can do this we shall come to just conclusions.

As the Lord is infinite love and wisdom, His final end in the creation of the material universe and of intelligent beings, must be the communication of happiness to them in the largest measures and the most excellent forms. Love could have no other end and wisdom could provide no other means than those which would conduce in the most direct and efficient manner to its accomplishment. The human mind must be organized to receive the good the Lord desires to communicate, and every material and spiritual substance and form must be created and perfectly adapted to be an instrument in communicating it. There must be a perfect order according to which all things and beings are related, and a perfect method according to which they act and react upon each other. Everything which stands in this order, and acts according to the method prescribed in the Divine mind, is good; everything which is contrary to this order, and tends in any way to oppose and prevent the Divine purpose, is evil. Evil, therefore, is disorder in the relations and activities of the human and Divine forces; it is discord in their action and reaction upon one another; it is the inversion and perversion of the forms of the human mind which was created to receive life and power from the Lord. Its organic forms are distorted, and the influx of life from the Lord is obstructed. Instead of flowing on in smooth and orderly currents, filling every organic form of the mind with power, life, and delight, they are turned out of their course, the inmost forms of the affections obstruct them, react against them, and this collision of opposing forces causes disease, misery, and spiritual death.

Evil in the mind is caused in the same way as disease in the body. The mind or spirit is a body in the human form; it contains in distinct order all the organic forms within and without which belong to the material body. Life is not a mere idea or an emotion; it is a substance and force flowing into the arteries and nerves and veins of the spiritual body as the nervous fluid and the blood flow through the channels of the nerves and arteries of the material body. Disease, which is evil in the physical plane of man's being, is caused by the derangement, obstruction, or excessive and

abnormal action of some of the organic forms of the body.
The result is pain and weakness, and unless the normal order
which we call health is restored, the body becomes wholly
incapable of performing its functions, and the spiritual body
throws it off as we do a worn-out garment. Moral and
spiritual evil is of exactly the same nature in the spiritual
plane of our being, with only this difference in the results.
Spiritual death is not the actual dissolution of the spiritual
body. It is only such a change in its organization that it
does not act in harmony with the forces of life which operate upon it. It is like a weak or inflamed nerve, or a con-
gested muscle, or a constricted blood-vessel, or an ulcerated
fibre. The forces of life still press upon every part of the
spirit, as the light upon the eye or the atmosphere upon
the lungs. As the spiritual body is diseased, the forces
which give it life and preserve its existence, so far as they
gain entrance, are opposed, turned out of their course; the
vessels of the mind do not act in harmony with them, and
the result is spiritual weakness, blindness, fear, sorrow, and
those insane hallucinations which flow from the supreme
love of self and the world, and lead us to regard the dust
of sensual delights and the transitory possessions of natural
life as more precious than heavenly and imperishable treasures. The faculties of the mind become so deranged that
one wars upon another, and there is discord, confusion, dis-
traction, and the wildest conflict; or indifference, stupidity,
and unconsciousness of the most excellent and distinctly
human qualities of our nature. We even lose the noblest
and most beautiful features of the human form, and become
debased into reptiles and beasts.

In the degree that the organization of the mind becomes deranged and departs from the perfection of its origi-

nal order, all its relations to other human beings and to the
outward world are disturbed.  Here again the analogy between the spiritual body and the material body is perfect.
When the eye is inflamed, the light becomes a torment to
it; when its various parts are diseased, or so deranged that
they cannot act in harmony, the vision becomes dim, the
images of objects are no longer seen in their true form, and
all relations to the outward world are disturbed.  Analo-
gous results take place when the understanding, which is
the spiritual eye, becomes diseased.  When it is inflamed
by passion, all the laws of the Divine order appear distorted.  The Lord who is love and mercy appears as the
direst enemy.  It cannot bear the clear light of truth; it
can only see its shadows in distorted forms.  It cannot see
in man a brother who is to be loved and helped, and whose
interests are to be regarded and cherished as our own.  He
appears as an enemy, rather, whom we are to assail and
subject to our own will.  Hence arise the gigantic evils
of war which have stained the earth with blood, filled
nations with widows and orphans, with famine and pestilence, with desolation and woe.  All social strife, the
fierce competition between labor and capital, the destructive rivalries in every employment and phase of human
action originate in these insanities, and cause such misery
that men of cultivated minds seriously discuss the question
whether life, which the Lord intended to be full of con-
tentment, peace, and joy, is worth living.  The mind is so
darkened that it cannot see the higher uses and loveliest
forms of the material world, and the affections have become so torpid that they are unconscious of the finer attractions and harmonies which pervade nature, and which
were intended to lift us above the material plane of life,

13

and win our souls to a higher knowledge, to purer and more exquisite joys.

All evil of every degree and form is, in its cause, a departure from the Divine order into which man and the universe were created. You cannot conceive of a physical or a spiritual evil which it is possible for a human being to suffer which did not originate, and whose existence is not continued, by a violation of the Divine order organized and embodied in man. There is not a domestic or social evil, a corrupt influence, a foolish or wicked custom or practice which is not caused by some derangement and violation of domestic and social life. Labor is a weariness, a slavery, and a curse, because selfishness and worldliness make it so. Civil life has been the theatre of ambition, rivalry, hatred, cruelty, and deadly conflict from the love of power and glory; and even the church has been corrupt, ignorant, contentious, domineering, worldly, and neglectful of her high mission. The fiercest of human passions have found refuge and full scope for their exercise within her fold. Every human relation has been the subject of evil, and become so by a violation of those laws of the Divine order which, obeyed, would have made them ministers of good. Such is the nature of evil when regarded from the point of view of the Divine order.

But this is not the point of view of the natural, unregenerate man. Every human being has a supreme, dominant love, which is the centre of his life. That love is the end which he seeks, and to which he makes every possession, force, and circumstance bend; it is his watch-tower from which he observes everything within his horizon; it is his oracle which he consults in every undertaking; it is the standard by which he measures every value, and determines every relation. Everything is good which favors that love, every obstacle to its attainment is a misfortune; every man, woman, spirit, angel, and even the Lord Himself, is regarded as an enemy who opposes it. That love is the god we worship, and bow down to, and to whom we delight to sacrifice all that we possess. This prayer, " Deliver us from evil," is the constant aspiration of every man, woman, and child; of every devil and angel. He who loves himself supremely, offers it with devout and sincere devotion. He is not content with the prayer of the lips; he enters into his closet, and shuts the door upon every other motive, and prays in secret. The fire of self-love is constantly burning upon his altar. But he not only prays with his lips and his heart; he prays with his hands, and with every physical and intellectual faculty. Those who love the world supremely are equally loyal to their god, and devout in their worship. They observe no dead formalities, they employ no obsolete and useless rituals; they do not pray as the hypocrites except when they come into the churches; they do not expect to be heard for much speaking. Their hopes are based upon vigorous action.

But there is a fatal principle in their worship. They regard every being, possession, and relation from a wrong point of view; they estimate all values by a false standard which reverses the order, the quality, and use of every being and thing in the universe. They make the instrumental primary, as though a mechanic should worship his tools instead of using them to do his work; they mistake the shadow for the substance; they invert the Divine order in the universe and in the human mind, regarding that as first which the Lord made to be last; they esteem that the lowest which He intended to be highest, the most precious that which, weighed in the balances of infinite wisdom, is the least valuable.   They mistake the fleeting appearances and the wild illusions of the senses for the most substantial realities and genuine wisdom.   In a word, they put darkness for light and light for darkness; error for truth and truth for error; evil for good and good for evil.   They pray for that which, if obtained, will be their ruin, and ask to be delivered from the means and conditions which will secure their eternal joy and blessedness.

As we all are in some degree in this unregenerate state, and subject to these natural illusions, it is a question of vital importance how to gain the true point of view, and offer the effective prayer for deliverance from evil.   We must know what evil is when measured by the Divine standards, and how to escape from it.   We can only gain the right point of view and secure a perfect criterion of judgment by a knowledge of Divine truth.   We cannot find it in our own understanding, for that has become perverted, its vision impaired, its judgment warped by the influence of a depraved will.   We cannot find it in our natural desires and affections, for they are the offspring of the same blind and corrupt parent as the understanding.   We cannot find it in ourselves; we must go out of ourselves; we must rise above ourselves; we must deny ourselves; we must distrust our own judgment; we must go contrary to our natural desires.   We must go to the Lord and put our trust in Him.   We must learn Divine truth from Him, and then we must make it the guide of our lives.

This is old and trite advice, it may be said: Can you give no other?   No.   There is no other.   Divine truth is the sum and substance of the Divine order; it is the law of the creation.   Its principles are organized in the human mind; it is the Divine method of bestowing happiness upon man; it is the embodiment of the Divine harmonies; it has its origin in the Divine nature; it is the form of the Divine love and the embodiment of every principle of order and harmony; it is the path and the only path that leads to heaven and the Lord. What other directions can be given? There are no other that can be trusted. So far as our wills and affections become subject to the Divine truth they come into harmony with the Divine will, and our hearts beat in harmony with the Divine heart. We are in the currents of the Divine order, and we are lifted up and carried on in them toward the infinite ocean of Divine love.

We must, therefore, learn the Divine truth from the lips of the Lord as He has spoken it in the Sacred Scriptures? Have you ever thought of it in this simple, practical way? Have you ever seriously reflected upon the comforting truth that the sure way and the only way of gaining deliverance from every evil is clearly revealed in the Bible? Are you not indulging the secret hope, almost unknown to yourself, perhaps, that there is some other way?—that you can regulate your affections and guide your actions by false principles, and yet escape their consequences? The natural degree of the mind is the embodiment of false principles, it is immersed in evils and inflamed by them, and there is no hope of deliverance in any other way than that pointed out by Divine truth. We are spiritually blind; the truth alone can restore our sight. We have wandered from the true path, and are lost in the mazes of error; the truth alone can show us the way, because it is the way. We are wearied with labor; we are distracted by conflicting desires; our hearts are full of unsatisfied aspirations; we are sick and dying; the truth will lift our burdens, appease our longings, heal our diseases, and raise us up from the grave. Truth is the way that leads from confusion to order; truth is the light that shines with clear and steady radiance upon the way. Truth is power adequate to all our wants. Truth is freedom and health. Divine truth is order, and leads to every possible good. If, then, we desire to be delivered from evil, we must learn the way of deliverance, and that way is revealed to us in the commandments. It is a way so plain that "the wayfaring men, though fools, shall not err therein."

But, it may be said, there are so many conflicting opinions, theories, and doctrines concerning sin and salvation that we do not know which to believe. There is such a complicated maze of paths, each of which is declared to be the only true one, that we are lost in our efforts to find the way. But the Lord does not require us to adopt any special theory of salvation. He does not say that we must conform to any special ritual. The splendid and complicated offices of the Roman Catholic Church, and the hard and naked forms of the Quakers are alike powerless to deliver us from evil. The Lord has given us a few simple rules which every one can understand, and He tells us to follow them. He does not ask us to form opinions, or construct theories, but simply to do what He commands. He says to every one of us, "If thou wouldest enter into life, keep the commandments;" "Cease to do evil, learn to do well," and "Though your sins be as scarlet, they shall be white as snow; though they be red like crimson, they shall be white as wool."

Here then is the practical way to offer this prayer. We

must learn the truths which show us what our evils are, give us weapons to combat them, and then we must do what the truths teach us. This is so self-evident that it seems almost absurd to say it ; and yet it is necessary to say it, and if it could be said in a way to awaken attention and lead to action, it would move the world to its centre. " The children of this world," our Lord has told us, " are wiser in their generation than the children of light." If we desire to see how men who really believe in their religion pray to be delivered from evil, we have only to look around us, or to reflect upon our own motives, and the efforts we make to gain deliverance from evils which hinder the attainment of the ends we seek. Look at those who seek to excel in physical strength, the pugilist, the runner, the oarsman. How severe the training to which they submit ! How diligently they practise ! How rigid in their diet ! How vigilant in guarding against every evil which may endanger their success ! and how almost superhuman their efforts for victory. Think of those who excel in art or song, or stand foremost in the world as musical performers. The excellence they reach is only gained by years of constant devotion and practise. They put themselves under the direction of the best masters ; they shun the evils they point out, they follow the directions they give. They do not wrangle about opinions, they do not complain that the lessons are difficult ; they do not expect to gain perfection by one effort. They are content if they find some advance from month to month. Look at those who seek for place or power, the devotees of fashion and pleasure ! How they labor ! what sacrifices they make ! what devotion they practise ! How loyal they are to the god they worship !

We may learn from them how to offer this petition and seek deliverance from the evils of sin and error. The mere utterance of the words has no power. We must learn what our specific evils are one by one. A general acknowledgment that they do exist will not save us. We must put our finger upon one and another, and avoid it. We must fight against it and try to overcome it as we would strive to overcome any false method or evil practice in our natural work. We must watch the tendencies of our affections and desires, the currents of thought into which we easily glide and delight to indulge. If we find them selfish, worldly, or evil in any of their tendencies or forms, we must change them. They are the effects of our spiritual enemies, who are constantly on the watch to work our ruin, and they are near us and their presence affects us because they find something in our natures which is congenial to them. They have found their way into the citadel of life, and we ought to take alarm at once and vigorously resist them. We must watch against them, and when discovered we should drive them away with the scourge of Divine truths as our Lord drove those out of the temple who made it a house of merchandise.

Especially should we guard against giving form and permanence to any evil suggestions by word or deed. We cannot prevent evil thoughts and affections from entering the mind, but we can reject them when they do come, and refuse to act according to them. When we accept an evil affection or a false thought as our own and act according to it, we make it our own; we adopt it, and it becomes a part of our being, as the food we have digested and assimilated becomes a part of our material bodies. We have built a home for evil spirits to dwell in, a citadel in which they intrench themselves, and from which they sally forth to renew their attacks upon us. A wicked deed is not a simple and single thing by itself. It is the concretion and embodiment of innumerable evil forces which lie behind it and dwell in it. As a plant or a mineral contains myriads of forms and forces, and by the finer laws which interpenetrate all things and bind them together, is connected with all other material objects, so a false thought or a wicked deed is the embodiment of myriads of evil forces and evil beings, and it conjoins us with them. When we commit an evil deed we open the doors to a myriad of evil influences and permit them to become anchored in our natures. On the other hand, when we shun a wicked act, we shun, we reject, and repel the hosts of wicked spirits and evil influences which were the cause of it. When we do this we pray in a most effectual manner to be delivered from evil.

Man in and of himself has no power to resist the evil spirits who are seeking to destroy him. They can refute his arguments; they can draw him on into sin by allurements which he has no desire to resist; they can approve his scruples by convincing him for the moment that there is no harm in the evil they solicit him to commit; they can quiet his fears by keeping his attention fixed on the immediate delight, and concealing from him the more remote but inevitable consequences. Good resolutions, formed in our own strength, are no barrier to their power.

What then can we do? Must we remain passive? By no means. We must do what we would if we were in the presence of natural enemies who were too powerful for us. We must avoid the outward occasions of their influence. We must shun the companions who are their instruments; we must avoid the sights and sounds which they use to beguile us. We must fortify and arm ourselves with those Divine truths which take effect upon them. And when they make an assault upon us, we must call upon the Lord to protect and defend us. But we must not rely upon our own strength; if we do we shall utterly fail.

Our doctrines teach us that when we shun an evil in outward act, the Lord can remove the myriads of evils which lay behind it. When we shun evil we put ourselves into the Lord's hands; He can bring His Divine power to bear upon our spiritual enemies, and He can deliver us. But He can only work this deliverance for us as we co-operate with Him. When we do our part He will not fail to do His. It is a work on which hangs our eternal destiny. All other gains, all other deliverances are nothing. As we are cleansed from evil good will take its place. All the influences which disturb our peace and cause us pain will be removed. We shall be "delivered from the hands of our enemies and all who hate us," the angels will draw near to us, and we shall come more fully into the light, the joy, and the peace of heaven.

# XIII.

## THE LORD'S KINGDOM, POWER, AND GLORY.

---

"*For thine is the Kingdom, and the Power, and the Glory, forever. Amen.*"—Matt. vi. 13.

THE Divine Prayer which our Lord teaches all His disciples commences with acknowledging Him as our Father, and ends with the humble confession that the kingdom, the power, and the glory belong to Him, thus completing the circle of thought and life. The first conception of God should be an idea of Him as a wise, loving, tender Father. We should impress this idea upon our children; we should keep it fresh and clear in our own minds; it should enter into, qualify, and dominate every conception we form of Him as we advance in spiritual knowledge. It is a Father's name we should desire to hallow; it is a Father's kingdom we should desire to see established; it is a Father's will, kind and tender and solely regardful of our happiness, we should pray to have done on the earth of our natural minds and in all human relations, as it is done in heaven; it is to

203

a provident Father, and not to some abstract law or unfeeling official, we look for daily bread; it is to a Father's merciful heart, and not to some arbitrary and relentless tyrant, we appeal for forgiveness; it is a Father tried and true to whom we trust for help in the conflicts of temptation, and from whom we seek deliverance from evil, and it is to Him, to our Father, we are ready to ascribe the kingdom, and the power, and glory, forever. How beautiful and happy life would be if we could keep this conception of the Fatherhood of the Lord constantly in our minds!

The acknowledgment that the kingdom, power, and glory are the Lord's is a logical consequence from the preceding petition. When we are delivered from evil, and so far as we are delivered from it, we shall ascribe the kingdom, power, and glory to Him. We shall see that it is by His power we are delivered from evil; that His kingdom does come as the kingdom of evil is subdued and destroyed. Our Lord teaches us to pray for that which He desires and intends to grant. Let us, then, endeavor to understand what is meant by the kingdom, power, and glory of the Lord, and how we are to acknowledge in heart and life that they are His.

" For thine is the kingdom." A kingdom is a country or people governed by a king, or, when regarded abstractly, it is the government of a king. It is also one of the primary divisions of natural history, a province of nature, composed of distinct forms and subject to special laws, as the mineral, the vegetable, and the animal kingdom. Here, in the material world, we get a clear example and representation of what a kingdom essentially is. Theologians have taken civil government, with an arbitrary and irresponsible ruler at its head, as the true type of the Divine government. But nature is a better representative. It is a province of the Lord's kingdom, and in it we can see how He governs and works. We can see that everything, from the least to the greatest, stands in a perfect order, and proceeds according to immutable law. Nature is not first created by an almighty fiat, and then brought into subjection to an arbitrary will. It is evolved according to laws which it embodies, and which constantly operate.

The Lord's spiritual kingdom, which is composed of human beings, is created and governed in the same way. The Lord did not create men and then impose laws upon them. He created them in His own likeness and image. He embodied in them the laws and principles of His own nature. The human soul is the organized form of the Divine nature; it was made to be a receptacle of the Divine life and to live by a constant reception of that life. Human life is the Divine life in us in finite forms. Even when outward laws or commandments were given to men, as on Mount Sinai, or when they came from the Lord's own lips in the flesh, they were only a statement of the laws which had been enacted in man's nature. "The kingdom of God is within us." All its substances, forms, activities, principles, and laws are embodied in potency in every human being, and when our natures are developed into actual existence according to these laws and principles, we become a kingdom of God in its least form; we become units in that kingdom.

A heavenly society, whether on the earth or in the spiritual world, is a kingdom in a larger form. All the regenerated in heaven and the regenerating on the earth constitute the Lord's universal kingdom. But, as every plant is the embodiment of all the principles of the vegetable kingdom, so every human being contains within himself all the principles of the heavenly kingdom. This is a kingdom of immutable law, of absolute order, and perfect relation. All its motions are harmonies; all its activities tend directly with the most exquisite precision to accomplish the Divine purpose, which is the communication of the greatest amount of the purest happiness to man, to make man the embodiment of the largest and richest joys. Every substance, every force, every activity which conduces to this end belongs to His kingdom.

This is the kingdom we must acknowledge and for whose coming we must pray. To do this implies much more than is generally supposed. It stands in direct contrast and opposition to the kingdom to which we belong by natural inheritance. The natural degree of the mind which we inherit from our parents, and which is first established in us, is a kingdom of evil affections and false principles. They are organized in the natural mind. It is called the kingdom of this world, the kingdom of Satan, our kingdom. This kingdom must be destroyed, or brought into subjection to the kingdom of heaven. Both cannot exist together in active power in the same mind at the same time. "No man can serve two masters." The Lord's kingdom is a kingdom of order; Satan's is a kingdom of confusion; the one is a kingdom of harmony, the other of discords; the one is a kingdom of light, the other of darkness. Evil is the embodiment of all that is impure, low, vile, corrupt, and destructive; goodness and truth are the substance and form of all that is innocent, lovely, elevating, noble, and pure. Evil is the kingdom of death; the Lord's kingdom is the form and embodiment of life. It is a state of peace. In it "all things celestial and spiritual are as it were in their morning, in their spring-tide flower, that is, in their essential happiness."

We can see from this contrast the logical sequence of our text, "Deliver us from evil, for thine is the kingdom." The acknowledgment that the kingdom is the Lord's implies an entire change in the organization of our minds. It is properly called being born again; it is the creation of new heavens and a new earth within us. It is the entire reversal of our motives and ends of life. "Thine is the kingdom." It is easy enough to repeat the words, but difficult to comprehend the full force of their meaning, and still more difficult to utter them from the heart. It is denying ourselves; it is abdicating our kingdom; it is forsaking all we have; it is laying down our natural, evil life; it is praying, struggling, working to be delivered from evil, and to be introduced into the kingdom of order, truth, and love. "Thine is the kingdom" falls from the lips in a moment, without effort, and too often without thought or comprehension of its meaning. How difficult to say it with the understanding, and to adopt it as the sincere desire of our hearts and the aspiration of our lives! Can you conceive of a higher or nobler aim in life than to become an embodiment of the Lord's kingdom; to have all your intellectual faculties fashioned into the perfect similitude of the order and beauty of the Divine original; to have all the affections imbued with the Divine love and move in accord with the harmonies of the Divine order? We are all striving to gain something which we call good; we are all seeking to attain an ideal, if it is no higher than that of a brute. What is our aim? We can tell what we desire to obtain and possess. Have we any clearly formed and definite idea of what we desire to become? Reflect upon it.  By the knowledge we gain, the affections we ex-ercise, and the deeds we do, we are becoming a kingdom, a kingdom of evil with all its discords, malignities, darkness, deformities, vileness, conflicts, hopeless sorrow and endless agonies, or a kingdom of truth, order, light, harmony, peace, joy, constant attainment, and ever-increasing happiness. Let us set these two kingdoms distinctly before us.  It may help us to pray with our hearts as well as with our lips, " Deliver us from evil, for thine is the kingdom."

Having considered what a kingdom really is, we have gained the true point of view to understand what we ask when we say thine is "the power."  Every human being loves power.  We love to possess it, we love to exercise it. This affection manifests itself in infancy and childhood, it increases with age, "grows with our growth, and strength-ens with our strength."  Yes, we all love power ; and the Lord loves to have us possess it and exercise it.  He cre-ated us for this purpose.  Scientists resolve all material substances in their last analysis into force.  We may go still further, and resolve all human beings into the same substance.  What is a man or a woman but an organized force?  We call the various modes of motion of the mind and body faculties.  What is a faculty ?  It is organized power.  The eye is the faculty or power of seeing, the ear is the power of hearing, the lungs of breathing, the brain of thinking.  Every organic form in the body is a faculty or power.  The whole material body is a series and conge-ries, a kingdom of faculties, and when any one ceases to perform its functions we feel its loss.

The mind is organized in the same way as the body. The mind is a spiritual body, organized to live in a spiritual world, and to become the embodiment of spiritual power.

It corresponds to the material body, organ to organ, in the least and in the largest forms. Every intellectual faculty is an organ. It would be as impossible to gain ideas, to think, to know, to compare, to reason, and to understand, to exercise any affection, or to be the subject of any pleasurable or painful emotion without spiritual organs, as it is to see without eyes, to hear without ears, to breathe without lungs, or to perform any physical act without the organ devoted to that use. Man is an organized power in every plane of his being, spiritual as well as material.

But whence comes the power? How does it originate? What are the conditions of its possession and exercise? Man does not create himself. He did not form the wonderful series of organs which constitute the human body. He can destroy the eye, but he cannot make one. It is impossible, in the nature of things, for any being or thing to create itself. We see this when we look at the works of our own hands. Show a child a watch and tell it that the watch made itself, and it would see the absurdity of the statement in a moment. The supposition that any faculty of the human mind or body originates its own power is just as absurd. The organ does not create the power; nor does the power of which it is the form and instrument originate in it. The power of seeing does not originate in the eye. The eye of itself cannot see. The same is true of every faculty of the material and of the spiritual body. The organ is in itself merely a form for the reception of power. We talk of the power of an engine; when we do it, we speak according to the appearance, and not with scientific accuracy. The absolute truth is that the largest engine has no more power than the smallest, and that is none at all. It is made to receive and distribute power.

14

So it is with man in the spiritual as truly as in the material plane of his being. He is organized to receive power in manifold and miraculous ways, but not one particle of it originates in himself. It is a constant gift to him by the Lord; but it is so given that it seems to be man's own. So far as our consciousness is concerned, it is our own. We cannot feel its currents flowing into us. It seems to spring up spontaneously within and to make us independent beings.

The distinction between this seeming and the genuine truth is a most important one. It is the ground and possibility of all evil. All error and sin originate in mistaking the appearance for genuine truth and acting upon it. Man's fall from his original innocence was caused by this fatal mistake. Every evil originates in claiming that as our own which belongs to another, and this is the essential evil from which we should pray to be delivered. We ought not to attribute either good or evil to ourselves. Power in itself is neither good nor evil. It gets its quality from the use we make of it. All power originates in the Lord. He is omnipotent; that is, He has all power, and there is no other power but His. All the forces of nature and of human beings, are the Lord's power working in and by means of the forms He has created, and these forces are constantly given. This is a truth we are slow to acknowledge. We talk of the forces of nature, of the power of an engine, of the strength of materials, of intellectual and moral power, as though all these varied forms of force were inherent in the forms which manifest them. We attribute to the instrument the power of the principal; to the vessel the precious substances which it contains. We forget the Creator in our admiration of His works. We claim for our own the power which is His constant gift. Do you not see the terrible danger that lies in this illusion? Do you not see how it begets pride, vanity, arrogance, self-love, the lust of dominion? Do you not see how it arrays man against man, and causes suspicion, strife, hatred, and revenge? When we claim any intellectual or moral quality as our own, we desire to have our claim recognized, to have our merits acknowledged and appreciated. If they are not, we feel injured, wronged; angry and resentful feelings arise in our minds. Why will not others respect me? Why will they not accord me the place to which my talents, my wealth, my skill, my ancestry, my personal qualities or possessions entitle me? Does not this principle lie at the heart of all the antagonisms and conflicts, all the pain and misery of life? Look into your own hearts, and watch the movements of your own affections, and you will see.

Suppose, on the other hand, you saw and acknowledged that every capacity of every kind you possess was the gift of the Lord, would it not reverse all your ways of thinking of yourself and of Him? You may be beautiful in person; instead of being vain of it you would be thankful to the Lord for it. You may possess some peculiar talent in which you excel many others. Did you create it? Did you endow yourself with it? No; it is the Lord's gift, and if you recognized His hand in it, instead of claiming superiority for yourself, you would be humble and grateful to the Lord for it. But the multitude will say we have no special gifts of excellence or superiority over others. How does the principle apply to us? In this way. Every power you possess is the Lord's free gift to you: it is His power constantly operating in you. Take the lowest form of His gifts, which multitudes regard as the highest. You can enjoy a good dinner. Who gave you the power of taste? Did you originate it? You can see and hear. Who formed the eye and the ear and constantly gives them the power to perform their functions? You are a mother and love your child. Did you endow yourself with this power? You are a mechanic. Who gives you the power to make a shoe or to build a ship or an engine? You are a merchant. Who gives you the power to buy and sell? You are an artist. Whence comes your skill? You are a student. Who gives you the ability to learn, to remember, to know, to understand? The Lord, the Lord, and He alone. It makes no difference through what channels the gift comes, it is the Lord's. The smallest, the commonest, as well as the largest and the rarest, is the gift of our Heavenly Father. Suppose we kept this grand and living truth before us, and our hearts were sensitive and quick to respond in every activity, in every enjoyment, in every acquirement, "Thine is the power"! Would it not keep us near to the Lord? Would it not fill our hearts with gratitude and draw us closer to Him? Would it not keep us under the shadow of His protecting wings where He could guard us against all harm? Think of it as you go the round of your daily duties. Think of it in the quiet joys of home. Think of it in social and public life. Think of it in all you suffer or enjoy, "Thine is the power."

But this phrase in the Divine prayer does not stand alone: it is most intimately connected with what precedes and follows it. The Lord not only gives us all the power we possess but He desires to give us more. There is no limit to the power He desires to bestow upon us, but it can only be done according to the laws of His kingdom. His kingdom is the method He has provided to bestow His gifts upon man, and there is no other way in which they can be given or received. How can the Lord give us the faculty of sight except by means of the eye, which is one of the provinces of His kingdom? How can He give us the power of hearing except through the ear, which is the kingdom of harmony? How can He give us the power of knowing in any other way than by the intellectual faculties; by memory, thought, reason, perception? How can He confer upon us the power of loving, with all its joys and exquisite delights, without the kingdom of the affections? There is no other way. The Lord's kingdom is the organized form and infinitely wise method by which He bestows His blessings upon man. Only, therefore, as we are inserted into this kingdom and become a part of it, can the Lord bestow His power upon us. " I am the vine," He says, " ye are the branches, He that abideth in me and I in him, the same bringeth forth much fruit; for severed from me ye can do nothing." All power and life, all capacity for sensation, is as impossible to man when separated from the Lord's kingdom as growth and the production of fruit to the branch when severed from the vine.

Evil is not power, it is weakness. Error is not power, ignorance is not power; they divert it, and destroy man's capacity for receiving it. We know that this is true in natural things, why can we not acknowledge it in spiritual things? We love power and desire to possess it. Why cannot we see that the only way to gain it and enjoy it is to put ourselves into orderly relations with the source of it? The most stupid mechanic knows that he must keep his wheels in connection with the motive-power or they cannot do his work. The child knows that it must open its eyes to see. Why should men and women, intelligent in many ways, be so foolish and stupid as to believe that the Lord can confer upon them the power of seeing heavenly truths, and the charm, the grace, the bliss of heavenly joys, when they close the gates of their minds against the currents of the Divine forces which carry these blessings in their bosom?

We have no adequate conception of our capacities to become the receptacles and embodiment of the Lord's power. Our ideas of power are too material and physical. There is a popular maxim that knowledge is power; and so it is in one sense, and in another it is not. Knowledge does not create power; it only shows us where to find it and how to use it: how to adjust ourselves to its inflowing forces. Knowledge does not create the power of gravity, of steam, of electricity, of wind and wave. Herein we may find a solution of what seems to be a contradiction and an enigma. Our doctrines teach us that the more completely we confess that we have no power of any kind, that it all belongs to the Lord, the more powerful we shall become, because the Lord can give us more. Do you not see that this is the condition on which every step has been taken in utilizing what we call the forces of nature? The scientist and inventor do not claim any of the forces of nature as their own. They do not think of changing one of the laws of nature. On the contrary, they direct their efforts to discover what those laws are; how natural forces act; the paths they love to follow; their attractions and repulsions; and when they have discovered them, they adjust all their movements and mechanisms to their immutable laws. Their constant prayer is, "thine is the power," and their constant desire is to bring themselves into such lawful and friendly relations to this power that it can become their own ; and it does become their own just so far as they discover its secrets and adapt themselves to its laws.

The same principle rules in the spiritual realm of the Lord's kingdom. All spiritual power is the Lord's. All the power to know, to love, to enjoy, is the Lord's, and can only be communicated to man according to the immutable laws of His kingdom. If we acknowledge this as the scientist and inventor do in their plane of action, we should become endowed with a spiritual power of which we now have but little conception. If the prayer, " thine is the power," was as genuine, fervent, constant, and practical in the churches as it is in the halls of science, in the labora- tory, and the workshop, they would become endowed with a spiritual power which would soon make " the kingdoms of this world the kingdoms of our Lord and of His Christ." They would gain finer and higher qualities of power. But the love of self and the world will not say it. " Mine is the power" is their constant claim and the cause of all their weakness and their shame. Give up the claim ; it is false. It is contrary to all the laws of the Lord and of His kingdom. Confess in heart and thought, in speech and deed, " thine is the power," and just in the degree you confess it and desire that it should be so, will you become the embodiment of spiritual forces ; of the power to know the finer qualities of the Divine character ; to come into more intimate relations with the Source of all life ; to be- come imbued with a keen perception of the Divine goodness, and a richer, larger, higher embodiment of Divine love and wisdom. In our cold and torpid affections and feeble un- derstandings we get but the faintest and feeblest idea that there is infinite power at our service, power to overcome evil, to see the true, to enjoy the good, if we will but accept it. Here we stand poor, blind, dumb, torpid creatures, in the midst of an infinitude of riches offered for our acceptance; in a world of light if we will open our eyes to see it; in a universe of harmony if we will lend our ears to hear, and surrounded within and without by living forces for whose reception we have only to open our hearts. We will not go to the Lord that we may have life.

But we must pass on to a brief consideration of the next truth revealed in our text, For thine is the "glory." What is glory? How can we ascribe glory to the Lord? By glory is meant Divine truth, because truth is spiritual light which fills the heavens with splendor. There is nothing of self-love, or of a desire to be honored and worshipped in the Divine nature. The Lord does not desire to be worshipped and to receive honor and praise from men for His own sake, but for man's sake. When man is in humiliation he is denying himself, he is laying down his life, he is praying to be delivered from evil, he is opening his heart to the Lord. When he does this he puts himself in the Divine hands, and the Lord can fill his whole being with love and light. "Glory for the sake of self," says Swedenborg, "is grounded in self-love, and heavenly love differs as much from self-love as heaven from hell, and infinitely more the Divine love." Our Lord Himself says, "Herein is my Father glorified, that ye bear much fruit." To bear fruit is to bring love to the Lord and man down into actual life, and embody it in our words and deeds. Every man, however humble his position, however servile his work, is ascribing glory to the Lord if he acts from love to Him. Every woman, however obscure her position and apparently trivial her office, is praying "thine be the glory" in every phase of domestic and social life, if her heart is alive with love from the Lord which she is in the effort to transmit to others. A child honors its parents by learning their will and acting in obedience to them. So we honor and give glory to our Heavenly Father by learning His will and doing it. We give glory to the Lord by receiving the gifts of love and wisdom He is in the constant effort to bestow upon us. He desires to bless us, and when we allow Him to do it, we honor and glorify Him, just as we honor and praise a human being when we help him to effect his purposes. Therefore we offer this prayer when we receive the Divine truth into our wills and understandings. Divine truth is light itself; the more we receive of it the more luminous we become. The wisest angels are the embodiment of a glory which flows from them as light from the sun. This light is so intense and powerful that weak and inferior natures cannot bear it. Their faces shine with a glory surpassing our conception. We sometimes see men and women with luminous faces even in this world. The light of love shines in their eyes and flows from every feature even through the thick veil of the flesh. How dazzlingly brilliant must be the faces of those who have cast off the veil and who have become the embodiments of heavenly light! We get a hint of the possibilities of the regenerate spiritual body to receive and transmit the Divine glory from the description of the angel of the Lord who descended and rolled back the stone from the door of the sepulchre. "His countenance was like lightning, and his raiment white as snow."

Such is the nature of the kingdom, and the power, and glory of the Lord, and such are the rewards of ascribing them to Him. It is not, as you see, an unmeaning act; it is not a mere motion of the lips; it is not merely the humiliation and denial of ourselves. That may be the appearance, but, in reality, it is becoming the kingdom; it is receiving the endowment of the Divine power; it is becoming the embodiment of the Divine light, and shining with it; and it is the attainment of all these blessings forever.

What are we to understand by that word, forever? Does it mean without end? Yes; it implies that, and much more. But, strictly speaking, it has no direct reference to time. There is no time in the spiritual world. What, then, does it mean? Through the ages,—that is, from age to age, from step to step, in our advancement through every phase of life in eternity. We are to ascribe the kingdom, the power, and the glory to the Lord, according to the state of our love and the measure of our knowledge. The more completely we can do this the more fully and perfectly we shall become His kingdom, be endowed with His power, and illuminated with His wisdom. Amen. We can say it easily with the lips. Can we say it with the heart? Can we say it with the understanding? Can we say it in our deeds? Our life, and not our lips, will give the true answer.

# XIV

## THE LORD'S PRAYER, SUMMARY VIEW.

---

"*After this manner, therefore, pray ye.*"—Matt. vi. 9.

DIVINE truth is revealed to us in the Sacred Scriptures in a perfectly logical manner, and this order exists in the Divine nature, and in all the Lord's works. It is the form in which the human mind is organized, and according to which all its developments proceed. The relations of one truth to another are those of cause and effect. This logical sequence exists not only in the lowest plane of truth, where one event is followed by another, but it is a progression by distinct steps from inmost principles to outward effects. The first truth revealed is the cause, the germ, and all the particulars are evolved from that in orderly succession, as we see in every act of creation around us. There is, "first, the blade, then the ear, then the full corn in the ear." The prayer which our Lord taught His disciples is not a collection of unrelated petitions, like a book of maxims. Their order could not be changed without breaking up the coherence and weakening the spiritual force and life of the prayer. There is very little evidence of this essential coherence between one part and another in the letter of the Word. Regarded from without, from a natural point of view, there does not appear to be any essential connection between the parts and the whole. Subjects are often introduced which, in their natural meaning, have no relation to what precedes or follows them. But this is owing to the Divine manner in which the Word is written. The natural acts and objects mentioned are signs of spiritual truths which are revealed by them. The connection exists in the spiritual laws revealed, and the natural expressions are connected by means of the spiritual laws embodied in them, and not directly with one another. We find a perfect illustration of this fact in every plant. The leaves, blossoms, and fruit are not connected with one another by outward contact, but by inward paths which originated in the germ.

Such being the manner in which the Word is written, we must try to get the central point of view and regard every particular from that; then we can see the relation of the parts to the whole and the whole to the parts. We have considered the various petitions of the Lord's Prayer separately; let us, in conclusion, regard them in their connections and relations, and get, as far as possible, a comprehensive view, collecting the rays of each particular truth into a focus, and pouring the concentrated light upon all.

" Our Father." These are the first words, and they reveal the central truth. They direct the mind to the Divine Person to whom we must direct our prayers, and in one word teach us how to regard Him. He is our Father. The idea is so familiar and simple that the little child can gain some true conception of it, and so comprehensive and profound that the highest angel cannot fully fathom and exhaust it. It includes all parental qualities. It comprises fatherhood and motherhood both. It teaches us that all wise and provident care, all gentle and tender ministries, originate in Him. It implies the deepest sympathy with us in all our sufferings and sorrows, help in our needs, forgiveness for our sins, and a love which changes not, and which desires to give itself with all its infinite riches to every human being. It is a conception of the Lord which commands respect, wins our confidence, and tends to draw out our affections to Him. He is our Father, not an almighty and inaccessible sovereign. The little child can go to Him with confidence and filial affection, ask its little blessings, and pour its little, transient sorrows into His patient ear; the ignorant can seek wisdom, the forsaken and lonely can find companionship, the widow and the fatherless protection and help.

This idea of the kind, tender, loving, wise fatherhood of the Lord must enter into our conceptions of all His relations to us. Is He in every principle of His nature opposed to evil and error? It is our Father who runs to meet and opens His infinite arms to the returning prodigal. Is He our Judge? A father's love enters into every decision and every sentence He pronounces. It is our Father whose name we must hallow, for the coming of whose kingdom we pray, whose will we seek to have done on earth as it is in heaven. It is our Father, and not some cold and heartless dispenser of public charity, from whom we ask our daily bread. It is our Father, loving, patient, forbearing, tender, and true, and not some inexorable tyrant, whose forgiveness we implore. It is a Father whom we beseech to stand by us in temptation, and deliver us from evil. It is a Father, our Father, to whom we ascribe all honor, power, and glory, in all states and conditions of life. Could we keep this loving, tender conception of the Lord in our minds, so distinct and powerful that it dominated every other, how delightful it would be to go to Him, to trust, to obey, to love Him!

But we are taught to think of Him not only as our Father, but as "our Father in the heavens," where we hope to find our eternal home. We are not to try to think of Him as some inconceivable essence above the heavens, but as "our Father in the heavens." There is something more important in this idea than merely locating Him in some place. He is in every truth and affection which constitutes heaven. He is in every pure affection, in every true thought, in every good deed; He is in every genuine good we enjoy. He makes heaven. He is the soul and life of all the sweet and lovely relations of the angels, of all their glowing activities, their glorious conceptions of the Divine nature, and the deep peace which fills their souls. Yes, He is our Father in the heavens, and will be forever.

With this idea of God clear in our minds, and the love which gives birth to it glowing in our hearts, we are prepared to say, "Hallowed be Thy name." It is not a dead formula; it is the spontaneous expression of our hearts. But what is the name of our Father in the heavens? It is the Lord Jesus Christ, the Divine Humanity which Jehovah assumed and by which He came into the world and redeemed His children from the hand of their enemies and saved them. Our Lord Himself declared, "I and my Father are one;" "I am in the Father and the Father in me;" "He that hath seen me hath seen the Father." And addressing

the Father, He says, "All mine are thine, and thine are
mine." By these words is expressed that reciprocal relation and personal unity which exists between the soul and
the body. In another place He declares, "The Father
dwelleth in me;" "No man cometh to the Father but by
the Son;" "No man knoweth the Father save the Son and
he to whom the Son revealeth Him." The Father and Son
are one person, as man's soul and body are one person; the
Father and Son are one God, as man's soul and body are one
man. The human nature assumed and glorified, or made Divine, made one with the Divine, became the embodiment of
all the Divine qualities in a form adapted to human comprehension. The Divine as it is in itself is above all finite
consciousness. In the Humanity it is brought down to
human conception. This truth is perfectly illustrated in
man himself. His unclothed spirit is above the power of
the senses. The spirit must be clothed with a material
body before it can reveal itself to other human beings in
this world. The material body is the man on the material
plane of being. The spirit dwells in it, and it dwells in
the spirit. It can say to the spirit, all mine are thine, and
thine are mine; no man can gain access to you but by me;
my name is your name and your name is mine.

But name implies much more than an epithet applied to
the Lord; it comprises all the Divine qualities, all the love
and wisdom of Jehovah, and the infinite variety of forms in
which they are embodied and manifested. To hallow our
Father's name, then, is to regard as holy and sacred all the
Divine attributes as they are revealed to us in Jesus Christ.
It is to revere His person, to cherish His spirit, to obey His
commandments, to follow His example. In doing this we
hallow our Father's name; we open our hearts to the re-

ception of His love; we receive His truth into our understandings, and we become more fully His children.

In the degree we hallow our Father's name His kingdom will come, and we shall desire to have it come with increasing power and glory. We regard as sacred the principles which constitute His kingdom; we love and adore the Being who is establishing His kingdom in the world and in human minds. In the degree we hallow our Father's name we place ourselves in such relations to Him that He can establish His kingdom in us; we open our understandings to the reception of the truths which constitute His kingdom. Whenever we regard a truth as supremely precious, every faculty of our nature seeks it, welcomes it, and cherishes it when gained. If it is a truth relating to our business, which teaches us how to succeed, with what joy we welcome it! How reverently we hallow it! How scrupulously we obey it! Suppose your father was sovereign of a rich and powerful kingdom which you were certain to inherit if you complied with some specified conditions. How eagerly you would seek to know the conditions! and when you had learned them, how faithfully you would preserve and obey them! They are your charter, your guide to power; they are the paths by which the kingdom comes to you. We can see how this principle operates in natural things, and how prompt the natural man is to hallow the name of every truth which will lead him to wealth and power. The same law governs in the spiritual realm. Our Father is a King; He is King of kings and Lord of lords. There are immutable conditions on which His kingdom will come to us, and we shall be endowed with its riches, power, and glory. The kingdom will come to us in the exact degree we hallow the name of our Father. The coming of the kingdom is the logical sequence and effect of hallowing the Lord's name.

" Thy will be done on the earth as it is in heaven." The Lord's will cannot be done until we know what it is. This is revealed to us in the truths which constitute His kingdom. We must, therefore, first learn the principles of His kingdom before we can do His will. This petition, therefore, follows in logical order from the preceding one. The Lord's will is His Divine love which is the purpose or end He constantly seeks. His kingdom is the government and order, and methods of His Divine wisdom. He seeks to establish His kingdom that it may become the embodiment of His love and the means of communicating it. He seeks to have His will done on the earth as it is in heaven. The Lord is in the constant effort to establish a heavenly kingdom on the earth. Heaven is heaven from the fact that the Lord's will is done in it. The societies of heaven are organized according to the Lord's will. Perfect order, subordination, and harmony reign there. It is the Lord's will that we should love Him supremely and our neighbor as ourselves. That is the law which reigns in heavenly societies. He teaches us to pray that it may be done in the earth.

This law of the Divine order has a personal application. The Lord teaches us to pray that His will may be done in the natural mind and on the earth of the material body as it is in the heaven of the spiritual mind. The Lord teaches us to pray that heavenly love may imbue all our natural affections, and purify and exalt them ; that heavenly wisdom may guide our thoughts and control our actions in our business, in our social relations, and in all the activities of natural life. We are to pray to have the natural mind and

15

our material actions dominated by heavenly principles. The practical and effective way to offer this petition is to apply it to ourselves, and to begin to do our part of the work in establishing the Lord's kingdom on the earth of our own natural minds. As men and women do this, the Lord's will will be done on the earth as it is in heaven. Civil governments will be organized in a heavenly form and public affairs will be conducted on heavenly principles ; domestic and social life will be reduced to heavenly order, pervaded by a heavenly spirit, and arranged in heavenly forms ; and grimy, servile, exhausting, ill-requited labor, will be animated by heavenly motives and become a form of heavenly use.

So far the petitions have looked directly to the Lord. We have asked nothing specially for ourselves. We are first raised to the highest, the inmost, the centre of all being, and from that point we begin to descend by means of the Divine Humanity, and according to the laws of the Divine order, to the earth. We return from the Lord to man, but, so far as we have offered the prayer with intelligence and sincerity, we bring with us the fatherhood of the Lord, and a reverent feeling for His holy name ; we have learned what that name is, and we have gained a distinct idea of our Father as a Divine man in the person of the Lord Jesus Christ. So far as we have gained any true knowledge of His Divine character and purposes, we are prepared and incited to ask that His kingdom may come and His will be done on the earth as it is in heaven. If we have any just conceptions of what this implies, of the immense changes which must take place in ourselves and in human society before His will can be done, and our agency in effecting it, we shall feel the need of Divine aid.

This leads us to pray, " Give us this day our daily bread."
As the Lord's will is done, we begin to see our dependence
upon Him, and our need of help. There is an immense and
difficult work put into our hands. It is the establishment
of a kingdom among a hostile people, against the power of
marshaled hosts, in the face of the most wily enemies ; it
is to be done with labor, and conflict, and pain ; with the
surrender of what we have held most precious ; we are to
take up the cross and even lay down our life. We have
occasion then to ask our Father to give us our daily bread.
As we begin to do our work in the establishment of His
kingdom, we shall gain a wider and higher idea of what is
meant by bread. The little child and the natural man may
regard it as food for the body only. But we shall soon discover that we need meat of a different kind of which the
body knows nothing, meat that will feed our souls, nourish
our affections and support us in our conflicts and labors in
preparing the way for the coming of our Father's kingdom.
As we begin to hunger and thirst after righteousness we
shall ask for the means of supplying our wants. As we
gain a truer knowledge of the Lord's kingdom and of our
relations to Him, we shall see that our life, and the means
of sustaining it, are a constant gift from Him, and we shall
go to Him with filial trust that He will supply our daily
needs according to their nature and degree.

The Lord's kingdom is to the natural mind as the sun to
the material world. As its organization advances and it
becomes established in our minds, its light dispels the darkness which has brooded over them, and reveals the diseased
and disorderly conditions of our affections and the distorted
forms of our intellectual faculties. " The light shineth in
darkness." Our true condition and relations to the Lord

are revealed. We are confronted with the terrible fact that, before we can really become the children of our heavenly Father, bear His image and likeness and become heirs of His power and glory, before we can hallow His name, before His kingdom can really come to us and His will be done on the earth of the natural mind as it is in heaven, there is a difficult and painful work to be done. This light reveals to us powerful enemies to be combated, evil and false principles to be eradicated, habits of thought and feeling and action which have become organized in our nature to be broken up. We awake to the fact that, instead of being children of our heavenly Father, and legal heirs of His kingdom, we are hopelessly insolvent debtors. Instead of claiming rights and enjoying possession, we must humbly supplicate for the forgiveness of our debts. Instead of being raised to heaven and taking our places in the Father's kingdom, of being clothed with princely apparel, and entering with shining faces into its noble activities, we must humble ourselves in the dust, we must confess our poverty, our indebtedness, our absolute dependence. Before the light for which we prayed came, we thought we were rich; now we find ourselves utterly destitute. Elated with the love of self and the world, we gloried in our independence; now we begin to see that we have no power of our own; every faculty and the ability to exercise it is a constant gift from the Lord. Where can we turn? What can we do? What else can we say than utter the Divine words which our Lord puts to our lips, " Forgive us our debts"? We are led to it by a logic of cause and effect from which there is no escape.

Suppose we have offered this petition with a sincere desire to have it granted. The Lord begins to answer it;

He begins to forgive us. But how? In the way we have asked Him; in the only way it can be done, and that is, "as we forgive our debtors." Now all our selfish and worldly loves are aroused. The mind becomes the arena of fierce conflicts. Wars are waged in it; earthquakes shake it; tempests of passion sweep over it; our hearts are rent with conflicting emotions; the mind is filled with confusion and pain and despair. This was not what we prayed for. We asked for forgiveness. We prayed to have our debts cancelled, and to become a member of the Lord's kingdom. We prayed for freedom and peace. Now we cry, O Lord, "lead us not into temptation." Save us from this conflict and pain. "Deliver us from evil."

Could we hear His answer it would be, "I am forgiving your debts; I am delivering you from evil. I am doing it in the only way in which it can be done. Your evil affections stand between you and heaven, and they must be subdued; they are enemies which must be driven out of the promised land before you can gain possession of it. The principles you have adopted as the rule of life are false; they are contrary to every law of my kingdom, and they must be rejected. 'You cannot serve God and mammon.' Sins cannot be uprooted, and the hard ground of the natural mind prepared for the seeds of heavenly principles without commotion and pain. You are a captive; you are in the hands of your enemies; you are a miserable slave, though they charm you by their illusions and persuade you that you are free. They promise you the kingdoms of the world, and the glory of them, and you have yielded to their enchantments. These illusions must be dispelled, and you must be rescued from their power before you can be delivered from evil. So long as you are wholly in evil you do not come into conflict. But when you seek deliverance from these enemies, then comes the conflict. My hand is in the struggle though you see it not. The pain which rends your soul is caused by the strain of heavenly forces withdrawing your affections from the grasp of your enemies. I am answering your prayer. Yield to me, and I will deliver you from all evil; I will forgive every debt; I will create you into my likeness and image; I will make you my child and heir to all my riches. The forgiveness of sin is not a remission of its penalties. It is the uprooting of its principles and the recreation of the human soul."

Suppose this work to have advanced so far that you can see its principles and necessary conditions. You see that the Lord's kingdom cannot be established in the human mind and His will be done on the earth of your own natural mind, or in human society, until the kingdom of evil and falsity is destroyed, and you begin to feel and to understand your utter helplessness to do this work alone. You see that you are a part of it; you are enslaved by its illusions, and subject to its dominion, and you can no more extricate yourself from its bondage by your own unaided power than you can change the organization of the material body, or the nature of the human mind. You are helpless in the toils of merciless enemies, and your Heavenly Father is the only being who can save you.

What would be the spontaneous utterance of one who understood the danger of his condition; the impossibility of escape from hopeless bondage by any power of his own, and who saw his bonds gradually loosening, the illusions disappearing, light breaking forth from the darkness, the hope of freedom and joy dawning, and who knew the Source from whence came his help? Would it not be:

"Thine is the kingdom and the power and the glory"? I owe my deliverance, I owe all I have and am to my Heavenly Father.

But the order and logical sequence of its parts is only one of the wonderful qualities· of this Divine Prayer. It is a golden key which unlocks the doors of the inmost closets of the mind and admits light and love from heaven. Swedenborg's experience of the wonderful power of this prayer is worthy of our attention, for his mind was consciously open to heavenly influences and a knowledge of the means by which they operate. The processes which go on in the secret chambers of the mind may be the same with others as with him, though we are not conscious of them. "While I was reading the Lord's prayer, morning and evening," he says, "the ideas of my thought were constantly open towards heaven, and innumerable things flowed in, so that I perceived clearly that the ideas of thought conceived from the contents of the prayer were filled from heaven. And such things were also infused, as it is impossible to utter, and also impossible for me to comprehend, only I was sensible of the general affection thence resulting. And what is wonderful, the things which flowed in were varied every day. Hence it was given me to know that in the contents of this prayer there are more things than the universal heaven is capable of comprehending; and that with man more things are in it in proportion as his thought is open towards heaven." Does not this give us a glimpse of the profound activities which may be going on in the secret chambers of the soul when we enter the closet and shut the door against selfish and worldly influences, and open it to the Lord? We pray to our Father in secret. We use the words He has given us, and we make them the vehicle of the desires of our heart. We perceive no powerful effects; the soul is not filled with exalted and glowing affections, the understanding is not flooded with light, because the operations are in secret. And yet the ideas of thought may be opened towards heaven, and innumerable things may flow in; influences may be exerted upon us which will have a controlling power in this life to protect us from evil and lead us to good. The highest forms of the will and the understanding, which are the most sensitive to the Divine forces, which give us our life, and which contain within them the promise and potency of every human endowment and attainment, are penetrated and imbued with life, the germs of heavenly affections are implanted in the will, and the power of perception, understanding, and thought is deposited in the intellect. The Lord draws nearer to us, gets a firmer hold upon the primary motives of life by means of which He can exert a more powerful control over our actions. We may have no conscious knowledge of these operations which are set in motion by a humble and reverent utterance of this prayer; but the germs of every good received in this act of communion with the Lord will come out into distinct consciousness when we pass into the spiritual world, and will give us new and larger capacities for the reception of the Divine life, create new forms, and add new charms to every relation and possession through the endless cycles of the ages.

We teach this prayer to our little children as soon as they are able to lisp it. It may not seem to us to be of much use. They can have only natural ideas of its meaning. But if we could see its real influence as revealed in the writings of the New Church, we should regard it of supreme importance. Speaking of the nature of an infant's mind in the other life, Swedenborg says, "At several different times, by the Divine mercy of the Lord, there were sent to me infants in choruses, and it was also granted to me to read to them the Lord's prayer, and at the same time it was given to perceive on such occasions how the angels in whose consort they were insinuated into their tender and novitiate ideas the sense of the things contained in that prayer, and filled their ideas according to their capacity of reception; and afterwards how it was given to the infants to think the same things as of themselves." Again he says, "While I was praying, the Lord's prayer and infants at the same time flowed into the ideas of my thought from their intellectual faculty, which was so tender that they scarce received anything but the sense of the words; nevertheless, it was manifest that their ideas in that state of tenderness were open even to the Lord,—that is, from the Lord; for the Lord flows into the ideas of infants in a more especial manner from the inmost plane of their being, inasmuch as nothing has as yet closed their ideas, as with the adult."

Do not these disclosures concerning the nature of the infant mind withdraw the veil and show us the power of this prayer, and the incalculable importance of teaching it to our children? While the mother with reverent and loving care is teaching it to her child and hearing it repeated by its innocent lips, angels are present who insinuate into its tender and sensitive mind the sense of the things contained in that prayer. A sphere of pure and heavenly influences flow from them which tend to mould the child's spiritual nature into heavenly forms, and to awaken in all its faculties heavenly activities. There is a power in this prayer of which we have no adequate conception. It is composed of living truths in a heavenly order. These truths are vessels for the reception of the Divine life, and when incorporated into the mind and cherished by the affections they are open to the Lord. Life from Him constantly broods over them, and according to their capacity flows into them, moulding them into the Divine image and likeness, arranging them into a heavenly order, and moving them to heavenly harmonies. It comprises all we need, all we can ask for, from the least to the greatest. It contains infinite things, because it is the embodiment of all the Lord desires to give us, and all that any created being can receive. Let us, therefore, teach it to our children; let us study it in its particular and related meanings; let us try to understand it, and to fill its ideas with genuine affection; let us repeat it with reverent hearts; let us ask the Lord to teach us how to pray it in an intelligent, fervent, and efficacious manner, that our affections may be penetrated and purified and exalted by its spirit, our understanding enlightened by its truth, and our actions guided by its wisdom.